Readers Theatre for Middle School Boys

Investigating the Strange and Mysterious

Ann N. Black

Illustrated by Cody Rust

Readers Theatre

Teacher Ideas Press

An imprint of Libraries Unlimited
Westport, Connecticut • London

Library of Congress Cataloging-in-Publication Data

Black, Ann N.
    Readers theatre for middle school boys : investigating the strange and mysterious / Ann N.
Black.
      p. cm. — (Readers theatre)
    Includes bibliographical references and index.
    ISBN 978-1-59158-535-0 (alk. paper)
    1. Children's plays, American. 2. Readers' theatre. I. Title.
    PS3602.L245R43   2008
    812'.6—dc22   2007034923

British Library Cataloguing in Publication Data is available.

Library of Congress Catalog Card Number: 2007034923
ISBN: 978-1-59158-535-0

First published in 2008

Libraries Unlimited/Teacher Ideas Press, 88 Post Road West, Westport, CT 06881
A Member of the Greenwood Publishing Group, Inc.
www.lu.com

Printed in the United States of America

The paper used in this book complies with the
Permanent Paper Standard issued by the National
Information Standards Organization (Z39.48–1984).

10 9 8 7 6 5 4 3 2 1

"Give them a good show!"

—E. R. B.

Contents

Acknowledgments

While developing this book, I received incalculable help from many places and many people. I thank them all most sincerely: Denise Welch for her ideas; Tutt Library of Colorado College and the Pikes Peak Library District for their generosity; the Pillar Players for their invaluable oral readings; my critique partners, Marty Banks, Linda DuVal, Maria Faulconer, Toni Knapp, and Susan Rust for their indomitable spirits and wisdom; Cody Rust for his inventive artwork; Hugh for "a' that"; and Dr. Casey Black for his untying-the-knots translation. Nothing would be possible or worthwhile without the constant confidence and support from my sons, Robert, William, and Casey. I extend my appreciation, also, to Elizabeth Budd and Sharon Coatney for their advice and editing done with such interest and patience.

Introduction

What is it about middle school boys? All that energy—that noise—that humor, curiosity, sensitivity—that drama!

If they're hooked into books, they're satisfying some of those urges. They settle down. They're quiet. They're discovering new worlds. They're tuning in to other emotions, real or imaginary. But drama? That's something else again.

Or maybe they're not hooked into books. That's when readers theatre comes in.

Traditionally, readers theatre implies that two or more oral readers present literature to an audience in a staged situation. *Readers Theatre for Middle School Boys*, however, uses as many boys as possible to present oral readings of strange and mysterious stories to their classmates on a stage that is either improvised or formal.

BENEFITS

The advantages for incorporating readers theatre into the Language Arts classroom of middle school boys are two-fold. Some are obvious; others are more subtle.

Readers theatre lessens the agonies of performing in public. Students can actually enjoy reading in front of others. The same benefit holds true for the teacher. She can enjoy producing a readers theatre program when everything works smoothly.

Simplicity is the key. A readers theatre performance can take place anywhere—in the classroom or on the stage in the auditorium. Unlike formal drama, a readers theatre performance does not need scenery or costumes. It requires no special lighting, no props, no music. Oral reading for performance needs intelligent and artful reading. That's all.

Memorization of the script is not a problem because every student on stage has a script with his part clearly marked and perhaps highlighted with yellow or blue. Being able to use a script onstage means that stage fright is rare.

These oral readers are not actors. There is no type-casting. Readers theatre does not discriminate because of physical appearance, such as height and weight or ethnic characteristics. Readers theatre calls only for oral reading skills and interest in the performance literature.

Any performance of readers theatre develops from team effort. The shy student is never alone on stage. Consequently, he gains more and more confidence. The show-off student becomes a part of the whole—he's shining, along with everyone else.

Subtle changes take place beyond the obvious advantages. Students delve deep into written language when they read aloud for others. They see how punctuation affects meaning. They see pauses and paragraphs as signposts they can't ignore. They discover the values in pacing, inflection, and the buildup and release of tension. They enlarge their vocabularies. Those funny words from other languages, maybe from distant times or strange people, suddenly acquire new meaning.

Oral readers soon realize that reading stories aloud to other people carries an unspoken message—responsibility for the audience. Recognizing this obligation, readers sharpen their communicative skills. They practice how to speak clearly and to project their voices. They learn how to use their eyes and hands effectively. They are able to respond with empathy to their fellow readers and thus heighten meaning and tone.

Accepting responsibility for the audience is a two-edged sword, however. Nothing of interest can affect the audience if the readers do not know everything possible behind the words they are reading. Research comes into play with dictionaries, biographies, and geographies.

For example, in one script, when Dr. Watson sees the speckled band wound about the villain's head, questions may arise about that snake—what can it do, where is it found, how does it kill? Or in Edgar Allan Poe's story, "The Masque of the Red Death," the horror may be increased even more following an investigation of worldwide, deadly plagues. Students will begin to read more, on purpose.

When the oral reader completely understands the words, emotions, and intent of a famous author, subconscious messages creep into the reader's own written language. Now when he writes, there is a spill-over. He is bound to think more about his own use of punctuation and his own choice of words for the ideas and emotions he wants to express. He thinks about the development of plot, as in "The Ransom of Red Chief." He follows the dramatic language that leads him to see that mysterious bear in *White Grizzly*, and to hear the Green Knight challenge Gawain.

The ten scripts in this book offer a wide variety of reading experiences for middle school boys. In addition, sound effects have been incorporated to take advantage of the inventive, adventurous nature of these young boys. Although the sound effects can be eliminated, they offer an extra dimension to the stories and provide extra opportunities for more students to participate. A full explanation for the sound effects appears in the Sound Appendix.

A PRÉCIS OF THE READERS THEATRE SCRIPTS

All of the scripts listed below were chosen for middle school boys who are anxious to investigate the strange and the mysterious in other worlds:

The Pied Piper of Hamelin, by Robert Browning, is an abbreviated version of the famous poem where rats and greed collide.

"The Adventure of the Speckled Band," by Arthur Conan Doyle, leads us and Dr. Watson to the untimely end of a villain, killed by his own snake.

White Grizzly, by Mary Peace Finley, follows the adventures of a young boy along the Santa Fe Trail as he seeks his true heritage.

Sir Gawain and the Green Knight is a modernized telling of the Middle English poem of fantasy, blood, and courage.

"The Ransom of Red Chief," by O. Henry, is the classic story of a young, obstreperous boy who gains the upper hand over his kidnappers.

"Sleepy Hollow," by Washington Irving, is a fanciful tale of the Headless Horseman.

"The Monkey's Paw," by W. W. Jacobs, brings us a story of greed and horror from an early, exotic India.

"To Light a Fire," by Jack London, is a story set in another time and another land with a hapless, ignorant, but sympathetic protagonist.

"The Masque of the Red Death," by Edgar Allan Poe, brings all of Poe's magic to an imaginary place where plague, ignorance, and selfishness cause disaster.

"The Country of the Blind," by H. G. Wells, is an unreal story that seems real—a fantasy of ambition, greed, and ignorance.

THE MORE THE MERRIER—OR EASIER

Generally speaking, facing a heavy line load alone can be a discouraging prospect for the young or inexperienced oral reader. Yet, many famous stories have little dialogue. They are more likely to have paragraphs of descriptive narration. These stories may be classics, but the long passages tend to daunt neophyte readers. Dividing up the narrative allows more students to share in the challenge of understanding passages and gives many students an opportunity to participate in performance.

A quick glance at the first page of any of the above scripts shows the duplication of narrative parts. For example, the lines for Sherlock Holmes will be read by four students and for Dr. Watson, four, as well. Three readers share the Green Knight's lines—two handle Sir Gawain's. In Poe's story, eight readers manage the narration. The more students who can take part, the easier and the more enjoyable it will be for all.

PRELIMINARY NOTES FOR PRODUCTION

Each script begins with two introductory pages for the teacher. The background of the author sets the milieu for the literature, and any special technical considerations are pointed out here, as well—such as the exact number of scripts needed. Reproducing on three-holed paper allows students to snap their scripts into a folder or notebook. Using black folders for everyone gives a smooth, professional look.

Early on, the teacher will need to brief the class about readers theatre before the casting and the rehearsals actually begin. The teacher will also introduce the literary subject and the author of the chosen script and discuss the expected audience and the planned performance space. Together then, the teacher and her students outline the time frame for the rehearsals and performance.

Most of the roles in these scripts are meant for boys. Girls may be necessary in a few, but they can participate in others, especially as narrators. However, the lines in the scripts are divided fairly evenly among the all characters. Generally, it is a good idea to make temporary assignments of the parts at the first one or two read-throughs.

On the first page of each script, X marks the spot that designates possible positions of the readers. These staging suggestions consider the relative importance of the characters. For example, Sherlock Holmes and Dr. Watson, placed at the front of the stage, take precedence over the roles of Roylott, Helen, and Julia. In "The Monkey's Paw," the Wife and Husband share center stage, with the Narrators flanking them on either side.

STYLES AND EXPECTATIONS

Certain stage patterns and styles have developed for readers theatre. For example, once the show is cast and rehearsals are underway, the teacher may begin working with movement—getting the performers on and off the stage and perhaps experimenting as to when they should sit or stand during the performance. Usually, readers do not move about the stage. It will be their facial expressions and the use of their hands that bring emphasis to their reading.

By and large, readers focus their reading out front, over the heads of the audience. They may direct this focus to the center, to the right, or to the left, but they do not directly address the audience.

Clothing styles are generally simple, and oftentimes colors are coordinated. Flashy jewelry and other ornaments are discouraged because they become distracting for the audience. Some casts wear black T-shirts for a uniform look during performance.

When the cue is given for the performance to start, an imaginary curtain rises and the students file onstage. They take their places, open their scripts, then bow their heads. On cue, they raise their heads, and the show begins. When the performance ends, the readers close their scripts, bow their heads (as they hear that welcome applause), and file off stage. Success!

Reading literature aloud has brought literature alive. Obviously, readers theatre will be advantageous for the individual student, but such performances can energize a whole class, indeed, the entire middle school.

Robert Browning—A Literary and Romantic History

They met in 1845, two English poets already famous—Robert Browning and Elizabeth Barrett. Mutual admiration for each other's work had prompted an exchange of lengthy letters that led to their meeting, then to their secret marriage in 1846. Elizabeth Barrett Browning, world renowned for her poetry, died in 1861 at their home in Florence, Italy. Although grief-stricken, Robert Browning continued on, caring for their young son and growing in style and stature into one of the great poets of the nineteenth century.

Browning, who was born in England in 1812 and raised there, received a cosmopolitan view of the world from his parents, who were both intellectually and artistically inclined. He was given full reign to his father's extensive library, and he was able to travel and study abroad, visiting Russia and Italy in his twenties.

Early on, Browning displayed a talent for writing. By the time he was a teenager, he had written a volume of lyric poems after the fashion of Percy Bysshe Shelley. His subsequent volumes, however, were only moderately successful. Finally, following the advice of others, he began to write for the stage, but his plays were not well received.

Still, as Browning matured, he used these past literary efforts in the development of the dramatic monologues that established his lasting fame. The Browning Society was formed in England during his lifetime, and similar societies have flourished throughout the world, from Kansas to New York to San Francisco, where even today that society offers annual awards for original dramatic monologue poems.

Robert Browning never married again. He devoted himself to his son, Pen, and to his work. He died in 1889, at age seventy-seven, at his son's home in Venice.

PRODUCTION NOTES

Robert Browning synthesized all the great attributes of the Romantic poet with the worldviews of the Victorian in his unique poetry—the dramatic monologue. This abbreviated version of *The Pied Piper of Hamelin* shows Browning's mastery of the character-driven story in one long poem.

The poem, however, is an old poem, and may present several challenges for inexperienced readers: recognizing the occasional outdated spellings from Browning's pen, understanding unfamiliar words, and grasping the full meaning under strong poetic rhythms. To assist in these efforts, the original punctuation of the poem has been altered somewhat, and the lines have been divided up for easier reading. Occasional interpretative help is added, as in the use of the "Rat-echo."

An all-boy cast can read the poem, but Readers Two and Three, especially, might be assigned to girls. The script calls for a cast of twenty. (However, for a smaller cast, lines can be combined. For example, instead of five Townspeople, one or two can read those lines; instead of three Corporation members, one member. One Reader can handle the narration lines assigned to Readers 7, 8, and 9.)

Sound effects include rat noises, feet running, tapping on wood, door opens and closes, water sloshing, coins rattling, sounds of flute or penny-whistle, and the scraping of rock against rock. Although sound effects can be eliminated, suggestions for their use are in the Sound Appendix.

Number of scripts required for a full cast and crew: twenty, plus one for the teacher.

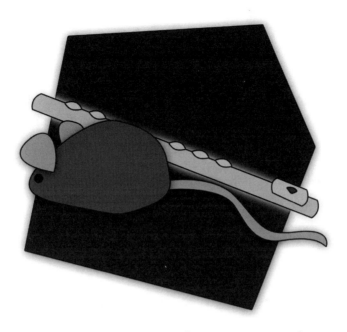

Rats and Fools

From *The Pied Piper of Hamelin* by Robert Browning

(Sounds) A, B, C, D			1, 2, 3, 4, 5 (Townspeople)	
X X X X			X X X X X	
Rat	Mayor	Piper	Rat-echo	Child
X	X	X	X	X
Readers 10, 11, 12			7, 8, 9 Readers	
X X X			X X X	

SOUND A: *(Slams book)* Rats! You didn't tell us our show is about poetry! Rats!

READER 11: Oh, come on, you can do it. This is about money—the golden guilder!

SOUND B: Okay, but we want something to sink our teeth into. Not poetry! Rats!

READER 11: Well, you might be surprised. Our poet is Robert Browning—and this poem is from a really old story—a legend from Transylvania.

SOUND C: Transylvania? That's not real. That's vampire country! Dracula! Frankenstein! Werewolves! Poets are namby-pamby!

READER 11: Really? What if I told you that this poet, Robert Browning, kept two skulls on his desk—one with a deadly spider living inside. (*Pause*) Do I have your attention?

SOUND D: You have mine!

READER 10: Okay. Let's begin—with a poem about vermin! Not maggots. Not lice. Not fleas. Rats! They were everywhere in Hamelin Town. Rats!

SOUND A, B, C, D: (*Squeaky sounds begin*)

MAYOR: Hamelin Town's in Brunswick—by famous Hanover city.

READER 11: The river, Weser, deep and wide, washes its wall on the southern side.

MAYOR: A pleasanter spot you never spied!

READER 12: But, when begins my ditty—almost five hundred years ago—to see the townsfolk suffer so—from vermin!—was a pity.

SOUND A, B, C, D: (*Few seconds of busy rat noises, high and low; gradually out*)

READER 5: Rats! They fought the dogs and killed the cats.

READER 2: And bit the babies in the cradles.

READER 12: And ate the cheeses out of the vats.

READER 2: And licked the soup from the cooks' own ladles.

READER 3: Split open the kegs of salted sprats, and made nests inside men's Sunday hats—and even spoiled the women's chats

READER 4: By drowning their speaking with shrieking

READER 1: And squeaking in fifty different sharps and flats.

READER 12: At last the people in a body to the Town Hall came flocking.

READER 2: "'Tis clear," cried they, "our Mayor's a noddy!"

READER 4: And as for our Corporation—shocking!

READER 3: To think we buy gowns lined with ermine for dolts that can't—

READER 1: Or won't, determine what's best to rid us of our vermin!

READER 2: You hope, because you're old and obese to find in the furry civic robe ease? Rouse up, sirs!

READER 3: Give your brains a racking to find the remedy we're lacking. Or—

READER 4: Sure as fate—we'll send you packing!

READER 10: At this, the Mayor and Corporation quaked with a mighty consternation. An hour they sat in council.

READER 11: At length, the Mayor broke silence:

MAYOR: For a guilder I'd my ermine gown sell. I wish I were a mile hence! It's easy to bid one rack one's brain—I'm sure my poor head aches again, I've scratched it so, and all in vain. Oh, for a trap, a trap, a trap!

READER 10: Just as he said this, what should hap at the chamber door but a gentle tap?

SOUND A: (*Gentle knocking on wood*)

READER 7: "Bless us!" cried the Mayor, "what's that?"

READER 10: (With the Corporation as he sat, looking little—though wondrous fat;

READER 11: Nor brighter was his eye, nor moister than a too-long-opened oyster—

From *Readers Theatre for Middle School Boys: Investigating the Strange and Mysterious* by Ann N. Black. Westport, CT: Teacher Ideas Press. Copyright © 2008.

READER 12: Save when at noon his paunch grew mutinous for a plate of turtle green and glutinous.)

MAYOR: Only a scraping of shoes on the mat? Anything like the sound of a rat makes my heart go pit-a-pat!

SOUND A: (*Gentle knocking on wood again*)

READER 8: "Come in!" the Mayor cried, looking bigger:

SOUND A: (*Door opens*)

MAYOR: And in did come the strangest figure! His queer long coat from heel to head was half of yellow and half of red.

READER 7: He himself was tall and thin—with sharp blue eyes, each like a pin.

READER 9: And light, loose hair—yet swarthy skin.

READER 8: No tuft on cheek nor beard on chin—but lips, where smiles went out and in.

READER 7: There was no guessing his kith and kin—and nobody could enough admire the tall man and his quaint attire. Quoth one—

READER 9: It's as if my great-grandsire, starting up at the Trump of Doom's tone, had walked this way from his painted tombstone!

READER 11: He advanced to the council-table. And "Please your honors," said he.

PIPER: I'm able (by means of a secret charm) to draw all creatures living beneath the sun (that creep—or swim—or fly—or run) after me, so as you never saw! And I chiefly use my charm on creatures that do people harm—the mole and toad and newt and viper. And people call me the Pied Piper.

READER 10: And here they noticed, round his neck, a scarf of red and yellow stripe to match with his coat of the self-same check—and at the scarf's end, hung a pipe!

READER 11: And his fingers, they noticed, were ever straying—as if impatient to be playing upon his pipe—as long it dangled over his vesture so old-fangled. "Yet," said he—

PIPER: Poor Piper as I am, in Tartary, I freed the Cham last June from his huge swarms of gnats.

READERS 7, 8, 9: (*Joint sighs and murmurs of "wonderful" and "amazing"*)

PIPER: I eased, in Asia, the Nizam of a monstrous brood of vampire-bats.

READERS 7, 8, 9: (*Murmers of "amazing!" and "Think of that!"*)

PIPER: And as for what your brain bewilders, if I can rid your town of rats, will you give me a thousand guilders?

MAYOR: (*Laughs*) One? One?!! *Fifty* thousand!

READERS 7, 8, 9: Fifty thousand!

READER 12: Was the exclamation of the astonished Mayor and Corporation.

SOUND A: (*Door opens*)

READER 11: Into the street the Piper stepped.

SOUND A: (*Door closes*)

READER 10: Smiling first a little smile—as if he knew what magic slept in his quiet pipe the while. Then, like a musical adept—

READER 1: To blow the pipe, his lips he wrinkled,

READER 2: And green and blue his sharp eyes twinkled,

READER 3: Like a candle flame where salt is sprinkled.

READER 4: And ere three shrill notes the pipe uttered—

SOUND C: (*Three high notes on flute or recorder*)

READER 4: You heard—as though an army muttered!

SOUND A, B, C, D: (*Rat sounds—begin with murmurs of low squeaks. Then squeaks deepen and become more agitated. Frantic scurrying sound—fingers on wood. Sounds continue under next twelve speeches.*)

READER 5: The muttering grew to a grumbling, and the grumbling grew to a mighty rumbling.

READER 1: And out of the houses the rats came tumbling!

READER 2: Great rats, small rats, lean rats, brawny rats, brown rats, black rats—

READER 4: Grey rats, tawny rats, grave old plodders, gay young friskers—

READER 3: Fathers, mothers, uncles, cousins; families by tens and dozens!

READER 2: Brothers, sisters, husbands, wives—followed the Piper for their lives.

READER 5: From street to street he piped—advancing,

READER 4: And step for step they followed dancing—

READER 1: Until they came to the river Weser.

READER 2: Wherein all plunged—

SOUND A, B, D: (*Noisy rat sounds stop*)

SOUND C: (*Sounds of rat bodies dropping into water, one at a time*)

READER 2: All plunged and perished!

READER 12: Save one who, stout as Julius Caesar, swam across and lived to carry to Rat-land home his commentary—which was. . . .

SOUND C: (*Flute stops*)

RAT: At the first shrill notes of the pipe, I heard a sound—as of scraping tripe—and putting apples, wondrous ripe, into a cider-press's gripe.

ECHO: Yum! Meat and ripe apples!

RAT: And moving away of pickle-tub-boards—

ECHO: He ignored the pickle-tub-boards!

RAT: And leave ajar of conserve-cupboards—

ECHO: Forget the jelly and jam. Leave open the conserve-cupboards!

RAT: And a drawing the corks of train-oil-flasks, and a breaking the hoops of butter-casks—

ECHO: Off with the corks on bottles of oil! Break open the casks of butter!

SOUND C: (*Flute again*)

RAT: And it seemed as if a voice called out, "Oh, rats, rejoice! The world is grown to one vast drysaltery!"

ECHO: Drysaltery? Drysaltery! The world is drying up?!!

RAT: "The world is grown to one vast drysaltery, so munch on, crunch on, take your nuncheon—breakfast, supper, dinner, luncheon!"

ECHO: Take your snacks—and your breakfast, supper, dinner, luncheon!

RAT: And just as a bulky sugar-puncheon, all ready staved—

ECHO: A sugar barrel already crushed?

RAT: A bulky sugar-puncheon, all ready staved—like a great sun, shone glorious—scarce an inch before me! Just as methought it said, "Come bore me. . . ."

ECHO: To bore a hole in the barrel? Incredible!

SOUND C: (*Flute stops*)

RAT: (*Nods*) Just as methought it said, "Come bore me!" (*Slowly, sadly, deliberately*) I found the Weser rolling o'er me.

SOUND B: (*Water sloshing*)

From *Readers Theatre for Middle School Boys: Investigating the Strange and Mysterious* by Ann N. Black. Westport, CT: Teacher Ideas Press. Copyright © 2008.

READER 10: You should have heard the Hamelin people ringing the bells till they rocked the steeple!

READER 9: "Go!" cried the Mayor, "and get long poles."

MAYOR: Poke out the nests and block up the holes! Consult with the carpenters and builders, and leave in our town not even a trace of the rats!

READER 12: When suddenly, up the face of the Piper perked—in the marketplace.

PIPER: First—if you please, my thousand guilders!"

READER 7: A thousand guilders! The Mayor looked blue.

READER 8: So did the Corporation, too—to pay this sum—

READER 9: To a wandering fellow with a gypsy coat of red and yellow.

READER 7: "Beside," quoth the Mayor with a knowing wink, "our business was done at the river's brink."

MAYOR: We saw with our eyes the vermin sink, and what's dead can't come to life, I think. So, friend, we're not the folks to shrink from the duty of giving you something to drink—and a matter of money to put in your poke.

READER 8: But as for the guilders. . . .

SOUND B: (*Coins being shuffled about*)

MAYOR: What we spoke of them, as you very well know, was in joke! (*Slight pause and then fake laugh*) Besides, our losses have made us thrifty. A thousand guilders! Come, take fifty!

SOUND B: (*Coins drop on wood*)

SOUND A: (*Decisive sound of gavel bangs twice*)

READER 10: The Piper's face fell, and he cried—

PIPER: No trifling! I can't wait! Beside, I've promised to visit by dinner time, Bagdad, and accept the prime of the Head-Cook's pottage—all he's rich in. For, having left in the Caliph's kitchen, of a nest of scorpions no survivor—with him I proved no bargain-driver. With you, don't think I'll bate a stiver! And folks who put me in a passion, may find me pipe after another fashion.

READER 9: "How," cried the Mayor, "d'ye think I brook being worse treated than a Cook?"

MAYOR: Insulted by a lazy ribald with idle pipe and vesture piebald? You threaten us, fellow? Do your worst. Blow your pipe there till you burst!

SOUND A: (*Door opens and closes*)

READER 1: Once more he stepped into the street, and to his lips again laid his long pipe of smooth straight cane.

SOUND C: (*Four high notes on flute or recorder*)

READER 5: And ere he blew three notes—there was a rustling—that seemed like a bustling of merry crowds jostling at pitching and hustling.

SOUNDS A, B: (*Patter of little shoes*)

READERS 2, 3, 4: (*Light, childish voices chattering excitedly. Light, happy clapping*)

READER 1: Small feet were pattering, wooden shoes chattering, little hands clapping, and little tongues chattering—and like fowls in a farmyard when barley is scattering—out came the children running.

READER 2: All the little boys and girls,

READER 3: With rosy cheeks and flaxen curls, and sparkling eyes and teeth like pearls, tripping and skipping, ran merrily after—

SOUND C: (*Soft notes on flute*)

From *Readers Theatre for Middle School Boys: Investigating the Strange and Mysterious* by Ann N. Black. Westport, CT: Teacher Ideas Press. Copyright © 2008.

READER 5: After the wonderful music with shouting and laughter.

READER 10: The Mayor was dumb.

READER 11: And the Council stood as if they were changed into blocks of wood, unable to move a step or cry to the children, merrily skipping by.

READER 12: Could only follow with the eye that joyous crowd at the Piper's back.

READER 11: But how the Mayor was on the rack, and the wretched Council's bosoms beat as the Piper turned from the High Street to where the Weser rolled its waters—right in the way of their sons and daughters!

READER 10: However—he turned from South to West, and to Koppelberg Hill his steps addressed. And after him, the children pressed.

READER 12: Great was the joy in every breast.

READER 5: He never can cross that mighty top!

SOUND C: (*Flute playing stops*)

READER 4: He's forced to let the piping drop.

READER 3: And we shall see our children stop!

READER 1: When, lo, as they reached the mountainside, a wondrous portal opened wide—as if a cavern was suddenly hollowed.

READER 2: And the Piper advanced and the children followed.

READER 5: And when all were in to the very last, the door in the mountain-side shut fast.

SOUND B: (*Slow grinding of rock against rock. Then rocks crash together.*)

READER 5: Did I say all? No! One was lame—and could not dance the whole of the way.

READER 4: And in after years, if you would blame his sadness, he used to say—

CHILD: It's dull in our town since my playmates left! I can't forget that I'm bereft of all the pleasant sights they see—which the Piper also promised me. For he led us, he said to a joyous land—

SOUND C: (*Flute plays very, very softly*)

PIPER: Joining the town and just at hand—where waters gushed and fruit-trees grew, and flowers put forth a fairer hue.

CHILD: And everything was strange and new. The sparrows were brighter than peacocks here, and their dogs outran our fallow deer.

PIPER: And honey-bees had lost their stings, and horses were born with eagles' wings.

CHILD: And just as I became assured my lame foot would be speedily cured, (*pause*) the music stopped.

SOUND: (*Flute music stops*)

CHILD: And I stood still—and found myself outside the hill—left alone against my will, to go, now limping as before, and never hear of that country more!

READERS 7, 8, 9: Alas! Alas for Hamelin!

READER 7: The Mayor sent East, West, North, and South—to offer the Piper, by word of mouth—wherever it was men's lot to find him—silver and gold to his heart's content—if he'd only return the way he went—

READER 8: And bring the children behind him!

READER 10: But when they saw 'twas a lost endeavor—and Piper and dancers were gone for ever, they made a decree:

SOUND A: (*Gavel pounds three solemn times*)

READER 11: That lawyers never should think their records dated duly—if, after the day of the month and year, these words did not as well appear:

READER 7: (*Solemnly*) And so long after what happened here on the twenty-second of July, thirteen hundred and seventy-six.

SOUND: (*Gavel pounds one decisive blow*)

READER 12: And the better in memory to fix the place of the children's last retreat,

READER 2: They called it—The Pied Piper's Street—

READER 3: Where any one playing on pipe or tabor was sure, for the future, to lose his labour.

READER 2: *Nor* suffered they hostelry or tavern to shock with mirth—a street so solemn.

READER 7: But opposite the place of the cavern, they wrote the story on a column.

READER 8: And on the great church-window painted the same—to make the world acquainted how their children were stolen away.

READER 9: And there it stands to this very day.

READER 10: And I must not omit to say (*Stage whisper*) that in Transylvania—

READER 5: There's a tribe of alien people—that ascribe the outlandish ways—

READER 1: *And* dress, on which their neighbors lay such stress, to their fathers and mothers—

READER 4: Having risen out of some subterranean prison—into which they were trepanned long ago in a mighty band—

READER 3: Out of Hamelin town in Brunswick land—

READER 2: But how or why (*Shakes head*) they don't understand.

READER 7: So, Willy, let you and me be wipers of scores out—with all men—

READER 8: Especially pipers! And whether they pipe us free from rats or from mice—

READER 9: If we've *promised* them aught, let us keep our promise.

SOUND A: (*Gavel bangs three times*) Now, there's a message to Browning's son. The Mayor and the Corporation didn't want to pay the Piper!

SOUND B: (*Shakes bag of coins*) I told you it was all about gold—filthy money!

SOUND C: Gold and wild imagination. It's a story! Well, I guess it's a poem.

SOUND D: Yeah? Well, I liked it. It's poetry—and I liked it! Robert Browning did a good job. It's poetry—but I liked it.

SOUND C: It was a story, okay? And it had a lot of old words. But it was okay.

READER 5: Promise and pride—all wrapped up in poetry—thanks to Robert Browning!

SOUND A, B, C, D: (*Squeaky sounds begin again. Flute begins.*)

ENTIRE CAST: Oh, no! No!

READER 12: They're back! Run for the hills!

READER 10: A new poet—quick!

READER 11: Find the piper. Pay him! I warned you!

SOUND A, B, C, D: (*All sounds stop. Folders close. Heads bow.*)

From *Readers Theatre for Middle School Boys: Investigating the Strange and Mysterious* by Ann N. Black. Westport, CT: Teacher Ideas Press. Copyright © 2008.

The Incredible Imagination of Sir Arthur Conan Doyle

Think of the Romantic poetry of Byron, Keats, and Shelley; of the caustic wisdom of Jonathan Swift; the realism of Dickens; the fantasies of H. G. Wells; then of the introduction of the detective story by Poe and Sir Arthur Conan Doyle. Easy enough to deduce, then, that in the 1800s the literary imagination shone with brilliance in Great Britain.

Straddling two centuries and two countries, Arthur Conan Doyle, born in Edinburgh, Scotland, on May 22, 1859, died in Sussex, England, July 7, 1930. Although knighted by King Edward VII for his support of the British during the Boer War in Africa, Doyle has been honored for more than one hundred years by a world of readers for his creation of Sherlock Holmes—a character he brought to life in detective stories that used observation and deduction to solve crimes.

Doyle's strong personal character is apparent in his devotion to his first wife, Louise Hawkins, an eventual victim of tuberculosis, and in his concern for their two children. His subsequent marriage to Jean Leckie and the birth of their three children strengthened his position and reputation as a loving and honorable family man.

Doyle's first career was as a doctor. He barely practiced medicine, yet he never gave up his interest in scientific matters or historical facts. Still, despite his affinity for the logical, his patriotic activism, and his familial obligations, for years Doyle harbored an intense interest in spiritualism, engaging in séances and believing in fairies, always seeking some kind of proof that life went on after death.

Certainly, Sherlock Holmes and Doctor Watson have achieved a unique kind of immortality. Springing from the imagination of Sir Arthur Conan Doyle, they have become quite real—human—to enthusiastic readers who clap their hands in belief and read on.

PRODUCTION NOTES

Sir Arthur Conan Doyle can be viewed as a classic study in contrasts. Respected as a responsible citizen and family man and as a prolific writer of romances, historical events, and patriotic issues, Doyle was beset with his attempts to understand the supernatural, even arguing his views with the famous magician, Houdini. However, despite these contradictions, Doyle's literary accomplishments were crowned forever by the sixty Sherlock Holmes mysteries he wrote, veritable studies in logic and reasoning.

Long before the current technical and scientific methods used in criminology—such as the matching of DNA or computer tracking—Sherlock Holmes used his mind to outwit the criminal's. Although the stories Doyle created begin with the backstory of a crime, readers always find the deduction and the re-creation of the crime vivid and exciting. These high points of the story, of course, need special attention when read aloud.

At these climactic points, we find the reading pace is slower, more intense, and more dramatic. The judicious inclusion of sound effects (though expendable) can also heighten excitement for the listener. If sounds are used, the Sound Appendix offers hints and suggestions.

The script calls for a total of seventeen readers, the storytelling being divided among Helens 1, 2, and 3 and Julia (parts for girls); and for boys, Roylott, Watsons 1, 2, 3, and 4; and Sherlock Holmes 1, 2, 3, and 4. Readers A, B, C, and D (either girls or boys) will open and close the performance, as well as handle the sound effects.

Needed for performance: a total of eighteen scripts and folders for the readers and the teacher.

"The Adventure of the Speckled Band"

by Sir Arthur Conan Doyle

Sounds A, B		Sounds C, D
X X		X X
Roylott	Helens 2,1,3	Julia
X	X X X	X
Watsons 2, 3, 4		Sherlocks 2, 3, 4
X X X		X X X
	Watson1	Sherlock1
	X	X

SOUND A: Pass me my deer-stalking cap. We're about to investigate a mystery!

SOUND D: Hold on. That's the famous Sherlock Holmes hat. Do you mean—?

SOUND B: Yes! I mean we're off on a hunt—with Holmes and Doctor Watson.

SOUND C: Off to solve a mystery—a puzzling, gruesome mystery—Sir Arthur Conan Doyle's Adventure of the Speckled Band. Go, Doctor Watson!

WATSON 1: Thank you very much. The events you mention occurred in 1883 when Holmes and I were sharing rooms as bachelors in Baker Street. One morning, I awoke very early to find Sherlock Holmes standing, fully dressed, by the side of my bed. "What is it," I asked, "a fire?"

SHERLOCK 1: No. A client. A young lady has arrived in a state of excitement. She insists upon seeing me. Should it prove to be an interesting case, you would, I am sure, wish to follow it from the outset.

WATSON 1: My dear fellow, I would not miss it for anything.

WATSON 2: I threw on my clothes and was ready in a few minutes to accompany my friend down to the sitting room.

WATSON 3: A lady dressed in black and heavily veiled rose as we entered.

SHERLOCK 1: Good morning, madam. My name is Sherlock Holmes. This is my intimate friend and associate, Doctor Watson. You can speak as freely before him as to myself. Pray, draw up to the fire, for I observe that you are shivering.

HELEN 1: It is not cold which makes me shiver. It is fear, sir. It is terror!

SHERLOCK 2: She raised her veil. We could see her restless, frightened eyes, like those of some haunted animal.

SHERLOCK 1: You must not fear. We shall soon set matters right, I have no doubt.

HELEN 1: Sir, I can stand this strain no longer. I shall go mad if it continues. I have no one to turn to. Oh, sir, do you not think you could help me?

SHERLOCK 1: I shall be happy to do so, Madam. And now I beg you to lay before us everything that may help us in forming an opinion upon the matter.

HELEN 1: Alas! The very horror of my situation lies in the fact that my fears are so vague, and my suspicions depend so entirely upon small points.

SHERLOCK 1: I am all attention, madam.

HELEN 1: My name is Helen Stoner. I am living with my stepfather, who is from one of the oldest Saxon families in England, the Roylotts.

HOLMES 4: (*Nods head*) The name is familiar.

HELEN 2: The family was, at one time, among the richest in England.

HELEN 3: Nothing is left—save a few acres of ground and Stoke Moran, the two-hundred-year-old house, crushed now under a heavy mortgage.

HELEN 1: My stepfather took a medical degree and established a large practice in Calcutta—but in a fit of anger, he beat his native butler to death.

HELEN 2: He escaped a capital sentence, but he suffered a long imprisonment.

HELEN 1: While living in India, he married my mother, a young widow, when my twin sister, Julia, and I were only two years old.

HELEN 2: When we returned to England eight years ago, our mother died in a railway accident. She bequeathed her money, a considerable amount, to Dr. Roylott entirely while we lived with him, with a provision—

HELEN 3: A certain annual sum should be allowed to us in the event of our marriage. Soon, Dr. Roylott abandoned

From *Readers Theatre for Middle School Boys: Investigating the Strange and Mysterious* by Ann N. Black. Westport, CT: Teacher Ideas Press. Copyright © 2008.

his practice in London and took us to live in the old ancestral house at Stoke Moran.

HELEN 1: A terrible change came over him. He seldom left the house, save to indulge in quarrels with whoever might cross his path.

HELEN 3: He became the terror of the village, for he is a man of immense strength and absolutely uncontrollable in his anger.

HELEN 2: He had no friends at all, save the gypsies who encamped on our land.

HELEN 3: He has a passion for Indian animals, and he has, at this moment, a cheetah and a baboon which wander freely over his grounds.

HELEN 1: My poor sister, Julia, and I had no great pleasure in our lives. She was but thirty, yet her hair had already begun to whiten. She died just two years ago. It is of her death that I wish to speak.

HELEN 2: Visiting our aunt one Christmas, Julia met an officer and became engaged. But within a fortnight of her wedding—the terrible event!

SHERLOCK 1: Pray, be precise as to details.

HELEN 3: The manor house is very old, and only one wing is inhabited. Our bedrooms are on the ground floor. Of these, the first is Doctor Roylott's, the second my sister's, and the third my own.

HELEN 1: On the fatal night, Doctor Roylott had gone to his room early. My sister was troubled by the smell of the strong Indian cigars he smoked.

HELEN 2: She left her room, therefore, and came into mine, where she sat for some time, chatting about her approaching wedding.

HELEN 3: At eleven o'clock she rose to leave me, but she paused at the door.

From *Readers Theatre for Middle School Boys: Investigating the Strange and Mysterious* by Ann N. Black. Westport, CT: Teacher Ideas Press. Copyright © 2008.

JULIA: Tell me, Helen, have you heard anyone whistle in the dead of night?

HELEN 1: (*Shakes her head no*) Never.

JULIA: I suppose you could not possibly whistle, yourself, in your sleep?

HELEN 1: Certainly not. But why?

JULIA: Because during the last few nights I have always, about three in the morning, heard a low, clear whistle. I cannot tell where it came from—perhaps the next room, perhaps from the lawn. I thought I would just ask whether you heard it.

HELEN 1: No, I have not. It must be those wretched gypsies.

JULIA: Yet—if it were on the lawn, I wonder that you did not hear it also.

HELEN 1: Ah, but I sleep more heavily than you. (*Pause*) She smiled back at me and closed my door. Moments later, I heard her key turn in the lock.

SHERLOCK 2: Indeed. Was it your custom always to lock yourselves in at night?

HELEN 2: Always—for security. The doctor kept a cheetah and a baboon loose.

HELEN 3: It was a wild night. I could not sleep. I felt misfortune impending.

SOUNDS A, B: (*Wind begins. Rain begins.*)

HELEN 3: Suddenly amid the wind and the rain—the wild scream of my sister!

HELEN 2: I rushed into the corridor—and heard a low whistle.

SOUNDS B, C: (*Low whistle, followed by slam of heavy metal*)

HELEN 3: And then, a clanging sound, as if a mass of metal had fallen.

HELEN 1: My sister's door opened.

From *Readers Theatre for Middle School Boys: Investigating the Strange and Mysterious* by Ann N. Black. Westport, CT: Teacher Ideas Press. Copyright © 2008.

SOUND D: (*Door opens and slowly creaks back and forth through next line*)

HELEN 2: (*Slowly*) It swung slowly on its hinges.

HELEN 1: My sister appeared, her face blanched with terror, her hands groping for help. Her knees gave way. She fell to the ground, writhing in pain. As I bent over her, she shrieked out in a voice I shall never forget.

JULIA: Oh, my God! Helen! It was the band! The speckled band!

HELEN 1: She could say no more, only stab her finger toward the doctor's room. All efforts were in vain. She died without recovering consciousness.

SHERLOCK 1: One moment. What conclusions did the coroner come to?

HELEN 2: He was unable to find the cause of death.

HELEN 1: My evidence showed no possible entry into her room. It is certain, therefore, that my sister was quite alone when she met her end.

HELEN 3: Besides, there were no marks of any violence upon her.

SHERLOCK 2: How about poison?

HELEN 2: The doctors examined her for it, but without success. It is my belief that she died of pure fear and nervous shock.

SHERLOCK 1: What did you gather from this allusion to a band—a speckled band?

HELEN 2: Perhaps to the band of gypsies, or to their spotted headscarves.

SHERLOCK 1: (*Shakes head*) These are very deep waters. Pray go on.

 From *Readers Theatre for Middle School Boys: Investigating the Strange and Mysterious* by Ann N. Black. Westport, CT: Teacher Ideas Press. Copyright © 2008.

HELEN 1: Two lonely years have passed, and I, too, am to be married in spring.

HELEN 2: Two days ago, repairs began on the house. My bedroom wall pierced. I have had to move into the chamber where my sister died—to sleep in the very bed in which she died.

HELEN 3: Imagine then, my thrill of terror when last night, as I lay awake, I suddenly heard that low whistle.

SOUND B: (*Low whistle slowly fades in and then away*)

HELEN 1: I dressed, slipped out, and made my way to you—for your advice.

SHERLOCK 1: You have done wisely. Yet we have not a moment to lose.

SHERLOCK 2: If we come to Stoke Moran, would it be possible to see these rooms?

HELEN 1: As it happens, it is probable my stepfather will be away all day.

SHERLOCK 1: Excellent. You are not averse to this trip, Watson?

WATSON 1: By no means.

SHERLOCK 1: Then we shall both come. You may expect us early in the afternoon.

HELEN 1: My heart is lightened already. I shall look forward to seeing you.

WATSON 2: Dropping her thick black veil over her face, she glided from the room.

SHERLOCK 1: And what do you think of it all, Watson?

WATSON 1: It seems to me a most dark and sinister business. Yet, if the lady is correct, her sister must have been quite alone.

SHERLOCK 3: But when you combine the ideas of whistles at night, the presence of a band of gypsies, and when—

SHERLOCK 2: We have reason to believe the doctor has an interest in preventing his stepdaughter's marriage—and the dying allusion to a band—

SHERLOCK 4: And the metallic clang, which might have been caused by one of the metal bars that secured the shutters.

SHERLOCK 1: There is good ground the mystery may be cleared along those lines.

WATSON 1: I see many objections to any such theory.

SHERLOCK 1: And so do I. It is for that reason we are going to Stoke Moran today.

SOUND D: *(Door opens and bangs against wall)*

SHERLOCK 2: What in the name of the devil!

WATSON 2: Our door had been suddenly dashed open. A huge man stood there.

WATSON 3: So tall was he that his top hat actually brushed the cross bar of the doorway, and his breadth seemed to span it from side to side.

WATSON 4: A large face, seared with a thousand wrinkles, burned yellow with the sun, and marked with every evil passion, turned from one to the other of us, while his deep-set, bile-shot eyes, and his high, thin, fleshless nose, gave him the resemblance of a fierce old bird of prey.

ROYLOTT: Which of you is Holmes?

SHERLOCK 1: My name, sir. But you have the advantage of me.

ROYLOTT: I am Doctor Grimesby Roylott, of Stoke Moran.

SHERLOCK 1: Indeed, Doctor. Pray, take a seat.

ROYLOTT: I will do nothing of the kind. My stepdaughter has been here. I have traced her. What has she been saying to you?

SHERLOCK 2: (*Changing the subject*) It is a little cold for the time of the year.

ROYLOTT: (*Angry*) What has she been saying to you?

SHERLOCK 3: (*Again, changes the subject*) I have heard the crocuses promise well.

ROYLOTT: Ha! You put me off, do you? I know you, you scoundrel! You are Holmes, the meddler—the busybody!

SHERLOCK 1: Your conversation is most entertaining. When you go out, close the door, for there is a decided draft.

ROYLOTT: (*Furious*) I will go when I have had my say. Don't you dare to meddle with my affairs. I am a dangerous man to fall foul of!

SOUND D: (*Door slams shut*)

SHERLOCK 1: (*Laughs*) He seems a very amiable person. This incident gives zest to our investigation! Now, let's order breakfast before my next errand.

WATSON 1: It was one o'clock when Holmes returned after his research on the will of the deceased wife of Doctor Roylott and the estate's income.

SHERLOCK 1: Each daughter, when married, can claim a modest annual income from the estate. (*Pause*) But if both girls married, Roylott would have a mere pittance. (*Pause*) We shall call a cab, Watson, and I should be very much obliged if you would slip your revolver into your pocket. That and a toothbrush are, I think, all that we need.

WATSON 2: At Waterloo Station we caught a train, then hired a trap and drove for four or five miles to Stoke Moran where we met up with Miss Stoner.

WATSON 3: After ascertaining that Doctor Roylott was in town until evening, Holmes began his investigation with the bedroom shutters.

SHERLOCK 2: Hmm. My theory certainly presents some difficulties. No one could enter if these shutters were bolted. (*Pause*) Well, we shall see if the inside of the rooms throws any light upon the matter.

WATSON 4: We passed at once into the chamber where Miss Stoner's sister had met with her fate.

WATSON 2: Holmes drew up a chair and sat silent, while his eyes traveled round and round and up and down, taking in every detail of the apartment.

SHERLOCK 1: With what or where does the bell communicate?

WATSON 4: He pointed to a thick bell-rope which hung down beside the bed.

HELEN 1: It goes to the housekeeper's room.

SHERLOCK 4: It looks newer than the other things.

HELEN 1: Yes, it was only put there a couple of years ago.

SHERLOCK 2: Your sister asked for it, I suppose?

HELEN 1: No, I never heard of her using it.

SHERLOCK 3: Indeed. It seems unnecessary to put so nice a bell-pull there.

WATSON 4: He took the bell-rope in his hand and gave it a brisk tug.

SHERLOCK 1: Why, it's a dummy! It's not even attached to a wire. Very interesting. It's fastened to a hook just above the little opening for the ventilator.

HELEN 2: How very absurd! I never noticed that before.

SHERLOCK 2: What a fool a builder must be to open a ventilator into another room.

SHERLOCK 3: With your permission, Miss Stoner, we shall now carry our researches into Doctor Grimesby Roylott's chamber.

WATSON 3: Holmes walked slowly around, examining each and all of the pieces of furniture with the keenest interest. Then he tapped a large iron safe.

SOUND C: (*Sound of pencil, perhaps, tapping iron.*)

SHERLOCK 1: What's in here?

HELEN 1: My stepfather's business papers.

SHERLOCK 4: There isn't a cat in it, for example?

HELEN 1: No. What a strange idea!

SHERLOCK 4: Well, look at this!

WATSON 4: He took up a small saucer of milk, which stood on the top of the safe.

HELEN 2: We don't keep a cat. But there is a cheetah and a baboon.

SHERLOCK 2: Ah, yes. A cheetah is just a big cat, yet a saucer of milk does not go very far in satisfying its wants, I dare say.

WATSON 3: Holmes squatted in front of a wooden chair, examining the seat with the greatest attention. Then he arose and put his lens in his pocket.

SHERLOCK 1: Hello! Here is something interesting!

WATSON 4: The object which had caught his eye was a small dog leash hung on one corner of the bed—but the leash was curled and tied into a loop.

SHERLOCK 1: What do you make of that, Watson?

WATSON 1: It's a common leash. But I don't know why it should be tied so.

SHERLOCK 1: That is not so common, is it? Ah, me! It's a wicked world, and when a clever man turns his brains to crime, it is the worst of all. Now, Miss Stoner, it is very essential that you follow my advice in every respect.

From *Readers Theatre for Middle School Boys: Investigating the Strange and Mysterious* by Ann N. Black. Westport, CT: Teacher Ideas Press. Copyright © 2008.

HELEN 1: I shall most certainly do so.

SHERLOCK 2: Good. When your stepfather returns, confine yourself to your room.

SHERLOCK 3: Then, when you hear him retire for the night, you must open the shutters of your window and put your lamp there as a signal to us.

SHERLOCK 4: Then withdraw quietly into the room which you used to occupy.

SHERLOCK 1: The rest leave in our hands. We shall spend the night in this room. We shall investigate the cause of this noise which has disturbed you.

HELEN 1: I believe, Mister Holmes, that you have already made up your mind.

SHERLOCK 4: Perhaps I have.

HELEN 2: Then for pity's sake, tell me what was the cause of my sister's death. Tell me whether I am correct—if she died from some sudden fright.

SHERLOCK 1: No, I do not think so. I should prefer to have clearer proofs before I speak, but I think there was probably some more tangible cause.

SHERLOCK 2: And now, Miss Stoner, we must leave you. If Doctor Roylott returned and saw us, our journey would be in vain. Goodbye, and be brave.

WATSON 1: Sherlock Holmes and I had no difficulty in engaging rooms at the nearby Crown Inn. They were on the upper floor, and from our window we could command a view of the Stoke Moran Manor House.

WATSON 2: At dusk we saw Doctor Roylott drive past and through the gates.

SHERLOCK 1: Do you know, Watson, I really have some scruples as to taking you tonight. There is a distinct element of danger.

WATSON 1: Can I be of assistance?

 From *Readers Theatre for Middle School Boys: Investigating the Strange and Mysterious* by Ann N. Black. Westport, CT: Teacher Ideas Press. Copyright © 2008.

SHERLOCK 1: Your presence might be invaluable.

WATSON 1: Then I shall certainly come.

SHERLOCK 1: It is very kind of you.

WATSON 2: You speak of danger. You have evidently seen more in these rooms than was visible to me.

SHERLOCK 2: No, you saw all that I did, but I may have deduced a little more.

WATSON 1: Holmes! I seem to see dimly what you are hinting at. We are only just in time to prevent some subtle and horrible crime.

SHERLOCK 1: Indeed. When a doctor goes wrong, he is the worst of criminals. He has nerve, and he has knowledge.

WATSON 4: The hours passed slowly away, and then at the stroke of eleven—

SOUND C: (*Clock begins to strike eleven, continuing under next two speeches*)

SHERLOCK 4: See! A single bright light from the middle window. Our signal to go!

SOUNDS B, C, D: (*Low sounds of wind*) (*Startling sound of baboon*) (*Footsteps*)

WATSON 1: (*Loud whisper*) My God! Did you hear that?

SHERLOCK 1: (*Low laugh*) It is a nice household. That is the baboon.

WATSON 2: Remember the cheetah, too!

WATSON 1: Arriving at the house, I felt easier when, following Holmes's example, I slipped off my shoes, and found myself inside the bedroom. Holmes noiselessly closed the shutters.

SHERLOCK 4: (*Whispers*) The least sound would be fatal to our plans. We must sit without light. He would see it through the ventilator.

SHERLOCK 3: *(Whispers)* Do not fall asleep. Have your pistol ready in case we should need it. I will sit on the side of the bed, and you in that chair.

WATSON 3: I took out my pistol and laid it on the corner of the table. Holmes had brought up a long, thin cane, and this he placed upon the bed beside him. By it, he laid a box of matches and the stump of a candle.

WATSON 2: Then he turned down the lamp, and we were left in total darkness.

SOUNDS B, C: *(Weird cry of a bird. Long-drawn cat whine. Distant muffled clock strikes one, pause, two, pause, three.)*

WATSON 4: Suddenly there was a gleam of light up in the direction of the ventilator—then the strong smell of burning oil and heated metal.

WATSON 3: Someone in the next room had lit a lantern.

WATSON 1: I heard the gentle sound of movement. Then all was silent.

WATSON 4: The smell grew stronger. For a half hour I sat with straining ears.

WATSON 2: Suddenly another sound—a very gentle, soothing sound, like that of a small jet of steam escaping continually from a kettle.

WATSON 1: Holmes sprang from the bed, struck a match, and lashed furiously at the bell-pull. Then he yelled!

SHERLOCK 1: You see it, Watson? You see it?

WATSON 1: I saw nothing—but I heard a low, clear whistle. The sudden glare of the match light made it impossible to see at what my friend lashed so savagely. I could see, however, that his face was deadly pale—and filled with horror and loathing.

WATSON 2: Suddenly there broke from the silence of the night the most horrible cry to which I have ever listened.

 From *Readers Theatre for Middle School Boys: Investigating the Strange and Mysterious* by Ann N. Black. Westport, CT: Teacher Ideas Press. Copyright © 2008.

WATSON 3: It swelled up louder and louder, a hoarse yell of pain and fear and anger all in the one dreadful shriek. (*Pause*) What can it mean?

SHERLOCK 1: It means that it is all over—and perhaps, after all, it is for the best. Take your pistol, and we will enter Doctor Roylott's room.

WATSON 2: With a grave face, he lit the lamp and led the way down the corridor. Twice he struck at the chamber door.

SOUND D: (*Two knocks on wooden door. Pause. Two more knocks.*)

WATSON 2: No reply from within.

WATSON 1: He turned the handle and entered—I at his heels, with the cocked pistol in my hand. (*Gasp*) It was a singular sight that met our eyes.

WATSON 3: On the table stood a lantern, throwing a brilliant beam of light upon the iron safe—the door of which was ajar.

WATSON 4: Beside this table, on the wooden chair, sat Doctor Grimesby Roylott. Across his lap lay the long leash we had noticed during the day.

WATSON 2: (*Slowly*) His eyes were fixed in a dreadful, rigid stare at the ceiling.

WATSON 1: (*Carefully, wonderingly*) And he had a peculiar yellow band, with brownish speckles, which seemed to be bound tightly round his head. As we entered, he made neither sound nor motion.

WATSON 2: I took a step forward. (*Slowly*) His strange headgear began to move!

WATSON 3: (*Scared*) And there reared itself—from among his hair—the squat diamond-shaped head and puffed neck of a loathsome serpent.

SHERLOCK 1: It is a swamp adder!—the deadliest snake in India. He has died within ten seconds of being bitten.

SHERLOCK 4: Violence does, in truth, recoil upon the violent, and the schemer falls into the pit which he digs for another.

WATSON 2: As he spoke, he drew the dog-whip swiftly from the dead man's lap, and throwing the noose round the reptile's neck, he drew it from its horrid perch, and carrying it at arm's length, threw it into the iron safe, which he closed upon it.

SOUND B: (*Decisive sound of heavy metal against metal*)

WATSON 1: There it is! (*Pause*) The true facts of the death of Doctor Grimesby Roylott of Stoke Moran. The little, which I had to learn of the case, was told me by Sherlock Holmes as we traveled back the next day.

SHERLOCK 1: I had come to an entirely erroneous conclusion, which shows, my dear Watson, how dangerous it is to reason from insufficient data.

SHERLOCK 2: I instantly had reconsidered my position on the gypsies. It became clear that the danger could not come from the window or the door.

SHERLOCK 3: The discovery that the bell-rope was a dummy—and that the bed was clamped to the floor—gave rise to a suspicion that more than the doctor's cigar smoke passed through that ventilator hole to the bed.

SHERLOCK 4: The idea of a snake—from India—instantly occurred to me. Its poison, of course, could not be discovered by any chemical test.

SHERLOCK 2: Then I thought of the whistle. Of course, probably with that milk, the doctor had trained the snake to return when summoned by the whistle.

SHERLOCK 3: He would put the snake through this ventilator with the certainty it would crawl down the rope and land on the bed. The occupant might escape every night for a week, but eventually she must fall a victim.

 From *Readers Theatre for Middle School Boys: Investigating the Strange and Mysterious* by Ann N. Black. Westport, CT: Teacher Ideas Press. Copyright © 2008.

SHERLOCK 4: The metallic clang heard by Miss Stoner was obviously caused by her stepfather closing the door of his safe upon its terrible occupant.

SHERLOCK 1: I heard the creature hiss as I have no doubt that you did, and I instantly lit the light and attacked it.

WATSON 1: With the result of driving it back through the ventilator.

SHERLOCK 1: And causing it to turn upon its master. The blows of my cane roused its snakish temper, so that it flew upon the first person it saw. I am no doubt indirectly responsible for Doctor Roylott's death. (*Pause*) I cannot say it is likely to weigh very heavily upon my conscience.

SOUND D: (*Shuts wooden door*) Excellent reasoning, Holmes!

SOUND C: (*Three strikes on the metal*) He solved the crime by deduction alone!

SOUND B: (*Brief notes on the whistle*) We deduce that the man is a genius!

SOUND A: Sherlock Holmes, master sleuth of The Adventure of the Speckled Band—one of sixty mysteries by Sir Arthur Conan Doyle. (*Pause*) Hey! Go read one!

From *Readers Theatre for Middle School Boys: Investigating the Strange and Mysterious* by Ann N. Black. Westport, CT: Teacher Ideas Press. Copyright © 2008.

Mary Peace Finley Spells Danger in *White Grizzly*

What a lucky little girl! Mary Peace Finley, a native of Colorado, grew up on the edge of history—along the Arkansas River near the site of Bent's Fort and the path of the old Santa Fe Trail. Her playground reached across the wide-open country and far into the nearby canyons with petroglyphs and pictographs, stone rings, pottery shards, and adobe ruins—mysteries to explore, contemplate, and write about in her stories and books.

However, today she confesses that as a youngster "history bored me—facts, names and dates. But touching history with my bare hands? That was awesome! History became real when I held a Native American clay pot that was about a thousand years old. Weaving this clay pot into a story that combines true events and people from history with the fictional adventures of people from my imagination all spells fun for me as a writer."

Sounds easy—but not so. Mary Finley's early school days were hampered by what she thinks today would be called dyslexia. She managed to overcome this handicap, graduate from the University of Denver, garner her indomitable perseverance and passion to write, and then began to write prize-winning stories for young people.

Every book in *The Santa Fe Trail Trilogy* has brought Finley prestigious awards from authors, teachers, librarians, publishers, and young people. Indeed, the third book in this series, *Meadowlark*, won the coveted Colorado Book Award.

An avid traveler, Mary Peace Finley has returned to her roots in Colorado, where she continues to pursue her hobbies and engage in further research and travel—yet she still finds time to give book talks, present lectures, and conduct writing workshops.

Above all, this extraordinary author continues to enlighten and enliven our lives with the love of history she weaves into her imaginative tales of the Southwest.

PRODUCTION NOTES

Mary Peace Finley's *The Santa Fe Trail Trilogy* offers readers Western adventures of a special sort, for the novels are peopled with the ubiquitous diversity that marked the opening of the West. Ethnic and moral differences ride side by side throughout, with the truth of history holding sway in every event.

These attributes also drive the drama in this script derived from *Soaring Eagle* and *White Grizzly,* the first two books in the trilogy. Historic Bent's Fort becomes virtually a character in these books, in addition to Native Americans, Mexicans, slaves, and traders. Together, they underlie a young boy's search for personal identity. Julio Montoya has been raised by a loving Mexican family, but he knows that he, somehow, is different. This script describes the beginning of Julio's quest to discover his real origin.

The script calls for a cast of thirteen, plus two members to handle sound effects. The five Narrators and Chivita (a dog) can be read either by boys or girls. Note: Narrator 2 has a questioning, somewhat naïve attitude. The other four are more straightforward in their descriptions and exposition.

Two characters in particular, Charlotte and Teresita, should be read by girls. The remaining parts, Dick, Papá, Red, Julio, and Bent, are male.

Two people can handle the simple sound effects, which include twigs snapping, harmonica music, a door opening, dishes and silverware rattling, a bell ringing, the sounds of a whistle and reed flute, puppy mewings, and a grizzly bear growl.

Sounds, though they heighten the dialogue, can be eliminated all together. Suggestions for these effects appear in the Sound Appendix.

Performing this script requires a total of fifteen copies, plus one for the teacher.

Mary Peace Finley Spells Danger in *White Grizzly*

	Sounds 1 & 2				
	X X				
Charlotte, Dick	Chivita		Papá	Red	Teresita
X X	X		X	X	X
Narrators 1-3	Julio		Narrators 4-5		Bent
X X X	X		X	X	X

NARRATOR 1: I hope you're not a squeamish lot.

NARRATOR 2: Squeamish? What is that supposed to mean? Scaredy-cats?

NARRATOR 1: No offense, but—yes, more or less. This story is not for sissies.

NARRATOR 2: (*Laughs*) Try us! Believe me, we can handle anything.

Excerpts from *White Grizzly* by Mary Peace Finley. Palmer Lake, CO: Filter Press, 2000; and *Soaring Eagle* by Mary Peace Finley. Austin, TX: Eakin Press, 1998. Reprinted with permission in *Readers Theatre for Middle School Boys: Investigating the Strange and Mysterious* by Ann N. Black. Westport, CT: Teacher Ideas Press. Copyright © 2008.

NARRATOR 3: Oh, right. That's what Julio thinks—until he faces that bear—a grizzly—somewhere along the Santa Fe Trail. (*Hoó-lee-o*)

NARRATOR 2: New Mexico, eh? Oh, I bet this is a long time ago. Right?

NARRATOR 3: Correct—going on two hundred years ago—way back when there was no *New* Mexico—just Mexico. Mary Finley writes about those days.

NARRATOR 2: Ah, *White Grizzly*. Okay, but what about this Julio—he's Mexican?

NARRATOR 1: Maybe. Actually, he doesn't know. His home is in Taos, Mexico. His family is Mexican, but he doesn't look like any of them. But why?

NARRATOR 3: Well, in *Soaring Eagle*, the day comes when he must travel to find out why. His goodbyes are painful, especially with his sister Teresita.

TERESITA: Oh, Julio, I know you want to go to Bent's Fort with Papá and make adobes with him. But that's not the only reason you're going, is it? It's what we've talked about before, isn't it? Your eyes, your hair. . . .

JULIO: (*Nods*) I can't keep anything from you, can I?

TERESITA: Yesterday—I asked Mamá again if you had another mother.

JULIO: What did she say this time?

TERESITA: She said, "No! Of course not!" So I asked her, what about his eyes? The rest of us don't have green eyes, or such light skin. Or hair the color of straw. And he's so tall. He doesn't look like any of us. "Well," she said, and gave me that look. (*Shakes her head. Sighs.*) Maybe she doesn't know.

JULIO: But if she doesn't know, who does? I've asked everyone!

Excerpts from *White Grizzly* by Mary Peace Finley. Palmer Lake, CO: Filter Press, 2000; and *Soaring Eagle* by Mary Peace Finley. Austin, TX: Eakin Press, 1998. Reprinted with permission in *Readers Theatre for Middle School Boys: Investigating the Strange and Mysterious* by Ann N. Black. Westport, CT: Teacher Ideas Press. Copyright © 2008.

TERESITA: I hope you will find out, Julio. I hope Papá can tell you—*will* tell you. Look—I want to give you this. It's a stone I found when we were little. (*Whispers*) It's a magic stone. Whenever I've been sad or lonely or afraid, I've held it for luck. Take it with you. When you hold it—will you remember. . . .

JULIO: Of course I'll remember you! We'll see each other again—and when we do, I'll give you back your stone, and you'll give *this* back to me.

TERESITA: Your tiny silver coin? You can't give this to me! Papá gave it to you.

JULIO: It's not a gift, just a trade—until we see each other again. All right?

TERESITA: (*Nods*) All right. And then you can tell me what you've learned—and what's out there beyond those mountains. May God protect you, Julio.

JULIO: And you, my sister. Adios!

NARRATOR 2: Looks like Julio is beginning his quest. Let's get going!

PAPÁ: So, Julio, you're ready, are you? It won't be an easy trip to the Fort.

JULIO: Yes. I know. (*Whistles*) Come, Chivita!

CHIVITA: (*Dog barks happily*)

PAPÁ: Where we are going could be dangerous.

JULIO: You've made the trip without trouble. Twice.

PAPÁ: Four times. Not always without trouble. Once we came close to being attacked by Arapaho.

NARRATOR 3: Papá's smile was grim as he inspected Julio's knife—just in case. But they soon left the green valley of Taos and began climbing the mountain trail north. On the second day, Papá led them off the trail.

Excerpts from *White Grizzly* by Mary Peace Finley. Palmer Lake, CO: Filter Press, 2000; and *Soaring Eagle* by Mary Peace Finley. Austin, TX: Eakin Press, 1998. Reprinted with permission in *Readers Theatre for Middle School Boys: Investigating the Strange and Mysterious* by Ann N. Black. Westport, CT: Teacher Ideas Press. Copyright © 2008.

PAPÁ: We'll camp here for the night. (*Whispers*) We'll be safer off the path.

NARRATOR 1: His father chose a place, but he did not gather wood for a fire. They ate a dinner of ground corn mixed with cold water from the stream.

NARRATOR 3: With their stomachs full, they leaned back against the tree trunks and huddled under their warm, woolen serapes. Then Papá began to talk.

PAPÁ: Julio—remember what I told you before—when I was nearly attacked by the Arapaho? I was young, like you, thirteen, fourteen years old. We were on a branch of the Santa Fe Trail, heading back to Taos. It was a blistering hot July afternoon. We all fell asleep in the cedars on a bluff above the trail—when Arapaho war cries woke us.

CHIVITA: (*Little doggy sounds of whimpering*)

JULIO: Sssh, Chivita.

PAPÁ: We thought we were dead for sure. (*Pause*) But the attack was below us on the trail.

JULIO: (*Whispering*) Papá, can't we talk about something else?

PAPÁ: Let me finish, Son. It's important to you. It's where your silver coin came from. Now, after the Arapaho rode off, we crept down to the wagon. Inside, the man and the woman were dead. A little girl, too.

JULIO: Why are you telling me this? Arapahos are as bad as Apaches. Apaches come down from the mountains to kill and steal! They're all savages! (*Pause*) I'm going down to the stream for a drink of water.

PAPÁ: Ah, Son, there are good people and bad people in every nation. What about the people in Taos Pueblo? The Cheyenne at Bent's Fort? (*Pause*) Julio—someone at the Fort now may know who the people in the wagon were. There was a little boy,

Excerpts from *White Grizzly* by Mary Peace Finley. Palmer Lake, CO: Filter Press, 2000; and *Soaring Eagle* by Mary Peace Finley. Austin, TX: Eakin Press, 1998. Reprinted with permission in *Readers Theatre for Middle School Boys: Investigating the Strange and Mysterious* by Ann N. Black. Westport, CT: Teacher Ideas Press. Copyright © 2008.

too—skinny little thing, all bundled up in a blanket in that blazing July heat. (*Laughs*)

SOUND 1: (*Twigs snapping*)

CHIVITA: (*Snarls*)

PAPÁ: (*Loud whisper*) Julio! Get down!

CHIVITA: (*Frantic barking*)

NARRATOR 4: Apaches! Julio froze. He searched frantically for a place to hide. Nothing—nothing but the bank of the stream. He flattened himself to the ground and rolled into the water, desperately grabbing on to a tangle of naked roots that trailed down into the stream.

CHIVITA: (*Barking and yelping, as in pain; grows louder, then fades away.*)

NARRATOR 2: Oh, no! When do the Apaches leave? Then? Or hours and hours later?

NARRATOR 5: (*Nods*) Finally. Then silence—and darkness. The cold of death crept up Julio's legs, into his body. Struggling in the quiet and the black, he pulled himself onto dry ground. Then, in the starlight, he saw—Papá.

CHIVITA: (*Low, mournful sounds*)

NARRATOR 4: Yet, despite the loss of his father, the wolves that come, the blinding snow, Julio fights to survive, and he holds onto Papá's last words—someone at the Fort may know who the people in the wagon were!

NARRATOR 5: Julio grows desperate—when he is found by the Cheyenne. Helped and healed by them, he again sets out on the Trail for Bent's Fort.

JULIO: Let's go, Chivita!

CHIVITA: (*Excited barks*) Eerp! Eerp!

Excerpts from *White Grizzly* by Mary Peace Finley. Palmer Lake, CO: Filter Press, 2000; and *Soaring Eagle* by Mary Peace Finley. Austin, TX: Eakin Press, 1998. Reprinted with permission in *Readers Theatre for Middle School Boys: Investigating the Strange and Mysterious* by Ann N. Black. Westport, CT: Teacher Ideas Press. Copyright © 2008.

NARRATOR 3: Bent's Fort rose from the prairie, tall and solid as rock, two stories high with double gates opened wide—as if in welcome. Julio slipped his reed flute into the leather bag at his side, straightened the shoulder strap, and wiggled his woven basket into place on his back.

JULIO: *Vamos*, Chivita! Come on.

NARRATOR 2: Is he going through those gates? I bet they'll stop him—and Chivita.

SOUND 2: (*Sound of music from harmonica*)

JULIO: *Hola!* (*Pause*) Hello?

SOUND 2: (*Music stops*)

RED: Hey! You can't go inside. Injuns trade there—at that window.

CHIVITA: (*Low, soft warning growl*)

JULIO: I don't have anything to trade. I came to see Mr. Bent.

RED: (*Slight laugh*) Mr. Bent is a very busy man, especially today. They call me Red. You can talk to me. What do you need?

JULIO: I'm Julio Montoya—the son of Enrique Montoya, the adobe maker from Taos.

RED: Enrique? You're Enrique's son? Hmmm. Well, follow me. I'll see.

CHIVITA: (*Soft, excited little barks*)

JULIO: Easy, Chivita!

SOUND 1: (*Door opens*)

NARRATOR 3: Julio had imagined the owner of Bent's Fort as a giant, but the man with dark hair and sunken eyes who was writing at a small wooden table was not a big man at all.

JULIO: Pardon me, Mr. Bent, for interrupting. I am Julio Montoya. My papá, Enrique Montoya, helped you build this fort. He was an adobe maker.

BENT: What? You're not Enrique's son. You can't be! With that yellow hair? And green eyes? Who put you up to this? Get him out of here, Red. Send him back to wherever he came from.

JULIO: I'm from Taos, Mr. Bent. And I *am* Julio Montoya! Enrique was my papá. He was carrying a message for you from your brother Charles.

BENT: Where's the message?

JULIO: Ay, no! Didn't you get it? After Papá—after the Apaches—I found the paper on Papá. I sent the message to you with a sheepherder.

NARRATOR 1: Bent began to sort through a stack of papers on his desk. When he held up the torn message stained with Papá's blood, Julio's stomach lurched, and he looked away. Bent read the message and put it down.

BENT: And you escaped all that. Well, I am sorry about your father, Julio. He was a fine man, an honorable man. I couldn't have built this Fort without him. Tell me, how old are you, anyway?

JULIO: I don't know—thirteen, maybe fourteen. But that's what I want to know! I want to know when I was born—and where!

BENT: Ah, yes. Yes.

JULIO: Just before Papá died, he said he found me near a burned-out wagon along the Santa Fe Trail. I was the only one left alive. Who were those people, Mr. Bent? Papá said someone here at your Fort knows. Did that person tell you, Mr. Bent? Do you know who I am?

Excerpts from *White Grizzly* by Mary Peace Finley. Palmer Lake, CO: Filter Press, 2000; and *Soaring Eagle* by Mary Peace Finley. Austin, TX: Eakin Press, 1998. Reprinted with permission in *Readers Theatre for Middle School Boys: Investigating the Strange and Mysterious* by Ann N. Black. Westport, CT: Teacher Ideas Press. Copyright © 2008.

BENT: I'm afraid I don't, Julio. I know your papá was proud of you. But until today I didn't know you weren't his own son.

JULIO: Excuse me, sir—but Mr. Bent. . . .

BENT: Out with it, boy. Speak up.

JULIO: Mr. Bent, I have to stay at the Fort until I find the man who talked with Papá. I don't have money to pay you, but I'll mix adobe, make bricks. I'll earn my way.

BENT: You want to work? That's good. You can ask around, too. See what you can find out. Now, go on—come back when Charlotte rings the dinner gong.

NARRATOR 2: Not going to be easy. Needle in a haystack? So many men to ask!

SOUND 2: (*Dinner table sounds*)

NARRATOR 3: Julio went on from one man to the other, asking—asking. Even at the dinner table he asked Mr. Bent's friends. One person overheard his story—Charlotte, the cook. And she came shuffling into the dining room with her husband, Dick.

DICK: Sorry, Mr. Bent, I reckon we should have waited until you finished eatin', but you know Charlotte! (*Laughs*)

BENT: (*Laughs*) That's all right. Julio—meet Dick and Charlotte Green from Missouri. Dick's our smithy, and Charlotte cooks for us.

SOUND 2: (*Dinner table sounds stop*)

DICK: We're real sorry about your daddy, Mr. Julio. We was good friends.

CHARLOTTE: We couldn't help from hearin' what you was jes tellin' these men. Your daddy tol' Dick that same story 'bout that man and woman in a wagon. White

	folk with two chillen, a girl and a towhead boy. And the boy was the only one left alive, poor li'l thing. Right, Dick?
DICK:	Yessum. Found that little one in July, Enrique said. That's why he named you Julio, 'cuz in Spanish that says July. And after Enrique tol' me about finding you, I tol' mah wife here and—
CHARLOTTE:	I remembered that ol' gentleman with the store in Independence, where Mr. Bent bought supplies 'fore we came here.
BENT:	Charlotte—you mean Myron Forester?
CHARLOTTE:	That's him! Forester's Mercantile.
BENT:	(*Shakes his head no*) Chance in a million.
JULIO:	What chance? What chance? Who is Myron Forester?
CHARLOTTE:	Like I said, he owns the store that outfitted us. Me and Dick was there so much, we got to know him. He tol' us about his son travelin' west with his family, a wife and two chillen, a boy and a girl. They—
DICK:	Disappeared—ten, twelve years ago! Mr. Forester's been askin' ever'body to watch for his family ever since. Said he'd wait ten more years. Your daddy—when I tol' him about Mr. Forester, he got real quiet. Finally, he said, "Julio should know about this. Soon."
JULIO:	So—so, is Mr. Forester my grandfather?
BENT:	Now wait a minute here. Enrique may have seen the similarity with Myron's story, but that doesn't mean there's any connection at all.
CHARLOTTE:	Don't you have nothin' from that wagon?

Excerpts from *White Grizzly* by Mary Peace Finley. Palmer Lake, CO: Filter Press, 2000; and *Soaring Eagle* by Mary Peace Finley. Austin, TX: Eakin Press, 1998. Reprinted with permission in *Readers Theatre for Middle School Boys: Investigating the Strange and Mysterious* by Ann N. Black. Westport, CT: Teacher Ideas Press. Copyright © 2008.

JULIO: A long time ago Papá gave me a little silver coin. I think he found it with the wagon. I left it with my sister in Taos—that's all I have, except this—something Mamá wrapped up in Papá's wool shirts.

CHARLOTTE: Why, honey—look at all that gold letterin'. This here's a Holy Bible!

BENT: A family Bible—in English? Why, this couldn't have been Enrique's!

NARRATOR 1: With the discovery of the Bible, clues unravel fast and furiously. Before long Julio discovers his true name, William Allen Forester—Billy—and his true birthplace of Mansfield, Pennsylvania—fifteen years ago. And he discovers he has a grandfather!—Myron Forester, waiting in Independence, Missouri.

NARRATOR 2: Yes, but waiting for only ten years. Julio—or Billy—better hurry up!

NARRATOR 3: First, Julio works for Mr. Bent, mending cracks in the adobe walls.

JULIO: Adobe always needs repair. Especially after rain, and it's rained a lot.

NARRATOR 3: Like his father'd taught him, Julio mixed dirt and river water into clay and patched the adobe walls carefully—until, one lucky day.

JULIO: Mr. Bent, are you taking that herd of sheep to Missouri? Chivita and I could drive them for you. We would earn our way.

CHIVITA: (*Excited little barks*)

JULIO: Quiet, Chivita. No *ovejas* yet. Quiet. (*o-ba-us*: sheep)

BENT: Chivita? You call that little dog *chivita*, little goat?

JULIO: Yes, sir. Papá suckled her to a goat so she'd be gentle with sheep. That's why we named her Chivita. She's the best sheep dog in Taos.

BENT: So—you and one sheep dog can herd all my sheep?

JULIO: Yes, sir. At home, we watched the sheep every night.

BENT: Well, I sure would like to get those sheep to my farm at Kansas Landing before winter. Hmm. You ever traveled with a wagon train?

JULIO: No, sir.

BENT: Days will be long, nights short. You've got to keep up. And you've got to understand one thing—the trail master is boss. His word is law. You do what he says. Agreed?

JULIO: Agreed. Who is the trail master?

BENT: (*Laughs*) I am! Soon as everything is loaded and the animals are hitched, we'll head on out. Tell Red to fix you up with supplies—and to hurry. You'll need everything. Now, go!

JULIO: Yes, sir. I'm on my way—to Red and to Missouri!

SOUND 1: (*A bell begins to toll. A whistle blows.*)

DICK: 'Mornin', Mr. Julio.

JULIO: Morning, Dick. Have you seen my dog? The wagon train's loaded and about to leave without me. I can't find Chivita. Have you seen her?

DICK: Well, Mr. Julio, maybe you ought to ask mah wife. (*Calls*) Charlotte! Charlotte? He's here!

CHARLOTTE: Well, 'bout time! That lil' ol' dog of yours—she's under the stairs in my room birthin' puppies!

CHIVITA: (*Soft doggy sounds*)

Excerpts from *White Grizzly* by Mary Peace Finley. Palmer Lake, CO: Filter Press, 2000; and *Soaring Eagle* by Mary Peace Finley. Austin, TX: Eakin Press, 1998. Reprinted with permission in *Readers Theatre for Middle School Boys: Investigating the Strange and Mysterious* by Ann N. Black. Westport, CT: Teacher Ideas Press. Copyright © 2008.

JULIO: Ah, Chivita—your very first puppies. But you scared me. I was afraid I'd lost you.

NARRATOR 1: Chivita was birthing six puppies—and Julio loved every one of them. Still, that meant some changes. Chivita and her puppies had to ride in the wagon. At first all went well on the trail. Dick drove the wagon, and Julio herded the sheep alone, waiting for Chivita to recover.

NARRATOR 2: Sounds too good to be true. Something bad is going to happen. I can feel it in my bones. Tell me I'm wrong.

NARRATOR 5: Sorry, can't do that.

NARRATOR 1: The first day went well, and on the first night Julio cut willow branches for a makeshift corral. He made his bed in the back of the wagon next to Chivita and her puppies. Dick slept near the fire.

SOUND 2: (*Soft flute music begins*)

CHIVITA: (*Soft little bark; puppy mewings*)

JULIO: Sorry to tie you to my ankle like this, Chivita, but I don't want you chasing after anything tonight. If trouble comes, I'll take care of it.

CHIVITA: (*Another soft bark or two*)

JULIO: Good night, Dick. Thanks for helping me today. When you get tired, call me for the next watch.

DICK: Good night. Jus' look at 'em stars, sparklin' like coals in a forge. Almost wish Charlotte was here with me. They sure be beautiful.

SOUND 2: (*Flute stops*)

NARRATOR 1: That was the last thing Julio remembered until Chivita was growling and tugging at the rope, struggling to jump out of the wagon.

JULIO: What is it, Chivita? Stay! Stay!

Excerpts from *White Grizzly* by Mary Peace Finley. Palmer Lake, CO: Filter Press, 2000; and *Soaring Eagle* by Mary Peace Finley. Austin, TX: Eakin Press, 1998. Reprinted with permission in *Readers Theatre for Middle School Boys: Investigating the Strange and Mysterious* by Ann N. Black. Westport, CT: Teacher Ideas Press. Copyright © 2008.

NARRATOR 3: Before his eyes could focus, Julio heard the high-pitched cries of a wounded lamb. His hand dived into his leather bag for his sling and stones—but they had no effect at all. Lambs screamed and bleated; their mothers brayed in protest.

DICK: I was watchin', Mr. Julio, but I didn't see a thing! What was it?

JULIO: Wolves maybe. Coyotes. Fox? Could have been a bobcat or a cougar. But look! The fence is down—and the sheep are running away!

NARRATOR 2: Oh, no! Now what? A whole herd of sheep scattering?

NARRATOR 1: Daybreak: splattered blood. Tufts of wool on the bushes. Lambs gone.

NARRATOR 3: Julio needs help from Mr. Bent and the men with the other wagons. He sends Chivita with Dick to round up the strays west and north.

CHIVITA: (*A little whine of protest*)

JULIO: *Ovejas*, Chivita. Go with Dick.

NARRATOR 1: Once Chivita understood, Julio turned away and walked to the east, following the tracks and watching—for rattlers, wolves, Apaches. Anything could be lying in wait. He paused once to look back.

NARRATOR 3: Chivita—she had stayed by his side almost constantly. They were like two halves of one whole. Now, even though they wouldn't be separated for long, he missed her.

NARRATOR 1: But nothing seemed dangerous here. He loped along the borders of cottonwoods that edged the Arkansas River and thought—of his family back in Taos, of the death of Papá—of the journey to Missouri that lay ahead of him.

Excerpts from *White Grizzly* by Mary Peace Finley. Palmer Lake, CO: Filter Press, 2000; and *Soaring Eagle* by Mary Peace Finley. Austin, TX: Eakin Press, 1998. Reprinted with permission in *Readers Theatre for Middle School Boys: Investigating the Strange and Mysterious* by Ann N. Black. Westport, CT: Teacher Ideas Press. Copyright © 2008.

NARRATOR 4: Suddenly he realized he hadn't seen any wandering sheep for at least a mile. Then—something rustled in the undergrowth.

SOUND 1: (*Twigs snapping*)

NARRATOR 4: He cupped a stone in his sling—but whatever had moved was too large to be a grouse or a quail. It could be a lamb.

NARRATOR 1: Julio crept forward—his moccasins scarcely making a sound.

NARRATOR 3: Then he froze!—not knowing why.

NARRATOR 1: Carefully—warily, he scanned the high weeds and grasses. Nothing.

NARRATOR 3: Nothing there—no one, but still that feeling. . . .

JULIO: Ay—it is nothing. Time to move—move along.

NARRATOR 1: Parting the weeds with both hands, Julio crept toward the movement in the grass.

SOUND 2: (*Deep, throaty growl*) Whuff!

JULIO: Ay—Dios!

NARRATOR 4: Five wagon-lengths away, a grizzly rose up from the tall grasses, its shaggy head wagging back and forth. It was feeding on a lamb.

NARRATOR 5: The grizzly peered at Julio with squinty red eyes—then it lifted itself up on its hind legs—higher and higher, until it loomed above Julio— sunlight glowing on the silver tips of fur.

NARRATOR 1: Every muscle in Julio's body screamed to run, but he didn't move—he would not look directly into the eyes of the grizzly.

JULIO: (*Whispers*) Ay, Santa Maria! Santa Maria—help me!

Excerpts from *White Grizzly* by Mary Peace Finley. Palmer Lake, CO: Filter Press, 2000; and *Soaring Eagle* by Mary Peace Finley. Austin, TX: Eakin Press, 1998. Reprinted with permission in *Readers Theatre for Middle School Boys: Investigating the Strange and Mysterious* by Ann N. Black. Westport, CT: Teacher Ideas Press. Copyright © 2008.

NARRATOR 4: The grizzly sniffed the air—wrinkled the bloody fur over its nose—showed the red, mottled gums and chipped, yellow teeth. Then it roared!—and the stench of its breath hit Julio like a putrid cloud.

JULIO: Ay. The slingshot will not help. My knife? No. A tree! My only chance is a tree! If I—step backward—very slowly—very slowly. . . .

NARRATOR 5: But then the grizzly charged!—so fast—so far that Julio was stunned.

NARRATOR 4: He spun around, tearing at the undergrowth, scrambling, running, stumbling—the bear close behind.

JULIO: A tree! A tree!

NARRATOR 4: He could hear the huffing—feel the heat rush from the grizzly's body.

NARRATOR 5: The first blow snagged him above his right elbow. He staggered, ducked, dodged to his left. He grabbed a tree trunk and swung around. His legs pushing, fingernails scratching, Julio shinnied up the tree.

NARRATOR 4: Roaring with fury, the grizzly reared. Sharp teeth closed around Julio's foot like a beaver trap.

NARRATOR 5: Screaming, Julio lifted his other foot and kicked with all his strength. He hit the bear's nose—his trapped foot jerked free, and Julio pulled himself higher into the branches, out of reach, but bleeding hard.

NARRATOR 4: Enraged, the grizzly swiped at the tree, then reared up once more.

NARRATOR 5: Clinging tightly to the tree, Julio grabbed a handful of leaves and plastered them tight against the wound, to stop the flow of blood.

NARRATOR 4: He felt his body growing weaker—dizzier with every moment.

Excerpts from *White Grizzly* by Mary Peace Finley. Palmer Lake, CO: Filter Press, 2000; and *Soaring Eagle* by Mary Peace Finley. Austin, TX: Eakin Press, 1998. Reprinted with permission in *Readers Theatre for Middle School Boys: Investigating the Strange and Mysterious* by Ann N. Black. Westport, CT: Teacher Ideas Press. Copyright © 2008.

JULIO: If I pass out, I'll fall. He'll have me. I'll die. Must do something. . . .

NARRATOR 1: Slowly, Julio peeled off his pantalones and tied the legs around himself and a branch.

JULIO: If I pass out, I won't fall into the mouth of the bear. Chivita! Santa Maria! Papá! Dick—Mr. Bent, help me! Come find me—soon!

NARRATOR 4: He drew out his knife. The claw wounds throbbed, his tongue was beginning to swell. He gripped the knife handle—tied his knife to the string of his white pantalones. The blade began rotating in the sun.

JULIO: Ay—it flashes. (*Weakly*) Flash. Flash. Flash.

NARRATOR 1: Julio forced himself to focus on the grizzly below—on the silver-white tips of its fur—on the huge, undulating form that rippled like water as it moved through the undergrowth.

NARRATOR 3: Then the grizzly seemed to separate from itself.

JULIO: Ay! Ay! Two grizzlies!

NARRATOR 4: One rushed toward the tree again, rising higher—closer and closer!

NARRATOR 5: It seemed to change—like a form hidden within a fog. It was huge now—glowing white—towering twenty feet above the ground—face to face with him. Its teeth were no longer jagged and broken.

NARRATOR 4: With a touch lighter than a feather, the grizzly's enormous forepaws encircled Julio and drew him close.

NARRATOR 5: Julio felt a jolt. He shivered. He seemed to hear a voice—one word from the past, the voice of his Cheyenne brother. (*Slowly*) "Protector."

NARRATOR 4: (*Slowly*) Then—like inhaled smoke—the white grizzly disappeared.

Excerpts from *White Grizzly* by Mary Peace Finley. Palmer Lake, CO: Filter Press, 2000; and *Soaring Eagle* by Mary Peace Finley. Austin, TX: Eakin Press, 1998. Reprinted with permission in *Readers Theatre for Middle School Boys: Investigating the Strange and Mysterious* by Ann N. Black. Westport, CT: Teacher Ideas Press. Copyright © 2008.

ENTIRE CAST:	(*Exhales slowly, audibly. Bow heads. After a moment, one head up.*)
NARRATOR 2:	You mean this is it? Protector? Protector? What does that mean?
ENTIRE CAST:	(*Heads up*)
NARRATOR 3:	(*Looks at Narrator 2*) Read the whole book! Read all three!—*Soaring Eagle, White Grizzly, Meadowlark.* Finley's the author, you know, Mary Peace Finley. Protector is her secret, but you can read all about it in *White Grizzly,* the book!
ENTIRE CAST:	(*Heads down again. End of show.*)

Excerpts from *White Grizzly* by Mary Peace Finley. Palmer Lake, CO: Filter Press, 2000; and *Soaring Eagle* by Mary Peace Finley. Austin, TX: Eakin Press, 1998. Reprinted with permission in *Readers Theatre for Middle School Boys: Investigating the Strange and Mysterious* by Ann N. Black. Westport, CT: Teacher Ideas Press. Copyright © 2008.

Strange Encounters with *Sir Gawain and the Green Knight*

We don't know exactly who wrote this wonderful story-poem. We have clues and suppositions, but nothing definitive. The original manuscript is thought to be more than six hundred years old, and it does exist—in the British Museum. In an effort to decipher its particular characteristics, scholars over the years have made a number of translations from its Middle English and have compared it to other literary works of this period.

The Gawain-poet, as he (or she?) is called, wrote in the unique poetic form of alliterative verse. For example, one stanza opens as, *"Wylde waye in pe worlde Wowen now ryde,"* or as it is in translation, "Wild ways in the world our worthy knight rides."

A general consensus holds that the poet, although probably a contemporary of Geoffrey Chaucer, was from a different part of England. Extant manuscripts of the two writers differ linguistically and culturally, as in their references to place and atmosphere. Chaucer was a product of southern England. The Gawain-poet seems to have come from the northwest part of the country, near Wales. Regardless of where the poet lived, the beauty, the humanity, and the excitement of the poem speak to us universally.

King Arthur, Sir Gawain, the Green Knight, and his lady are seen as flawed but courageous participants in a test of moral ethics. Challenge, temptation, and redemption all underlie the magic imposed by the mythical Morgan le Fay, tutored by Merlin.

An actual beheading takes place in the poem, another is threatened, and three seduction scenes contribute to the narrative excitement of the poem.

Echoes of a knight's trial and the embrace of a country can be heard today in the motto of the British honorary Order of the Garter: *Honi soit qui mal y pense*—"Shame to the man with evil in his mind."

57

PRODUCTION NOTES

Sir Gawain and the Green Knight, an alliterative romance poem, presents an ancient story to us in a style virtually unused today. The poem is thought to have been written about 1375. Its true origins and the identity of the poet have been extensively researched, but much still remains a mystery. Yet the poem continues to fascinate, and scholars such as J. R. R. Tolkien and contemporary poets such as W. S. Merwin continue to try their hand at translation.

This script, developed from a nineteenth-century translation, includes slight modifications for the modern young reader as, obviously, the vocabulary and linguistic structure of Middle English is quite arcane. The story is there, however, a romance in verse recounting the people and happenings of King Arthur's time—all with the striking use of alliteration. One note of warning: these repetitions do take careful oral reading.

The script calls for a cast of sixteen, plus one sound-effects person. Narrators 1 and 2 act as interpreters of events and terms—Narrator 2 asks the questions, and Narrator 1 answers. Lines for the Poet have been split into Poet 1, 2, and 3. Three readers can easily handle these speeches of description and narration. This splitting device is used for Green Knight 1, 2, and 3; Gawain 1 and 2; Arthur 1 and 2; and Guide 1 and 2. Lines for the Lady and the Porter have not been divided. Roles are available for both boys and girls.

Only a few sound effects have been added to the reading of the poem, but the sound of chopping off a head can certainly enhance a scene. The sound effects, of course, can be eliminated, but the Sound Appendix offers suggestions for their execution, for example, using an apple for the head.

In all, seventeen scripts (plus one for the teacher) will be required.

Strange Encounters with *Sir Gawain and the Green Knight*

Guide1 & 2		Lady		Porter Sound
X X		X		X X

Green Knight 1, 2, 3	Gawain 1 & 2	Arthur 1 & 2
X X X	X X	X X

Poet 1, 2, 3	Narrator 1 & 2
X X X	X X

NARRATOR 1: So are you ready for the spin back, sir—or lady, as the case may be?

NARRATOR 2: How far back? I get a little nervous when we talk Shakespeare.

From *Readers Theatre for Middle School Boys: Investigating the Strange and Mysterious* by Ann N. Black. Westport, CT: Teacher Ideas Press. Copyright © 2008.

NARRATOR 1: Further! Back to a magical mystery time—think King Arthur.

NARRATOR 2: Would that be real? Or unreal?

NARRATOR 1: Take your pick. Does anybody really know? But don't we all kind of believe it's true—the Round Table and those knights—like Sir Lancelot—and remember Sir Gawain? Take a listen to his story.

NARRATOR 2: Oh, I don't know. This sounds like the Dark Ages.

NARRATOR 1: Well, it might, but our story, this poem, comes from the Middle Ages, when a poet looked back in time—to when knighthood was in flower and the world was full of challenge and pride. Back to early Britain—to a time when a strange knight appears—is he real or unreal?

NARRATOR 2: I'm hooked. Let's begin. Ah—where would that be?

NARRATOR 1: Where else—but in Camelot? Hark, my friend, to the poet!

POET 1: King Arthur sat royally on the high dais at Christmastide, surrounded by many fine lords and the best of men—all the high brethren of the Round Table and their ladies.

POET 2: A feast they held at Camelot for fifteen days. A joyful din by day and dancing at night. It was a merry time with the noblest of kings.

POET 3: Sir Gawain, Arthur's nephew, sat nearby. And Queen Guinevere, with her dancing gray eyes, she, the most beautiful, in fine silk, sat in their midst under an embroidered canopy set with the finest of jewels.

POET 2: Good King Arthur would not eat till all the company was served. This was his custom.

POET 1: Nor would he eat until he had been told a tale of marvels, of ancient heroes, great battles, or other adventures. So he waited.

 From *Readers Theatre for Middle School Boys: Investigating the Strange and Mysterious* by Ann N. Black. Westport, CT: Teacher Ideas Press. Copyright © 2008.

POET 2: The first course came in with a blare of trumpets and merry melodies. Platters of fresh meats and stews followed. So many dishes!

POET 1: Then the music stopped for a moment. A new sound—a new noise!

POET 3: An awesome being had burst into the hall! In height—one of the tallest men in the world, square and thick from his neck to his waist. His limbs were so long and great, he seemed half a giant.

POET 2: Into the hall, this largest of men had come riding—and he was the handsomest of men, for though he was huge, he was well proportioned. But it was his color that amazed them all. This bold knight was entirely green.

NARRATOR 2: Are you serious?

POET 1: All green was this man—and his clothing. White fur trimmed his coat and his hood. Green were his stockings—his spurs of bright gold. All the rest was pure green with gold embroidery and beautiful jewels.

POET 3: All the metal was enameled. The stirrups he stood on were colored the same, and his reins glimmered and glinted all of green stones.

SOUND: (*Horse stomping. Light jingle of bells.*)

POET 1: The horse that he rode was of the same color, too—a green horse, great and thick, restless, matching the knight who rode him.

NARRATOR 1: Ssh. Not a word! Just believe—his horse is green, as well.

POET 2: Fair, flowing hair fell to the man's shoulders. His beard like a bush.

POET 3: The mane of the great horse was much the same, curly and combed, with knots of gold wire. The tail

From *Readers Theatre for Middle School Boys: Investigating the Strange and Mysterious* by Ann N. Black. Westport, CT: Teacher Ideas Press. Copyright © 2008.

and the forelock were twined with a band of bright green, set with jewels and bells of burnished gold.

POET 1: Such a steed! Such a hero that rides him—never before beheld in that hall. His glances, like lightning, it seemed no man could withstand.

POET 2: Yet he had no helmet, wore no armour, and carried no shield. Instead, in one hand he held a sprig of bright green holly. But, in the other hand, he carried a huge weapon—an axe.

POET 3: The blade was made of green steel and beaten gold; the edge, shaped for cutting, sharp as razors. The warrior gripped the shaft of the axe and rode straight to the dais—afraid of no one, and greeting no one.

GR.KNIGHT 1: Who governs this company? I would I see that hero—speak with him.

POET 2: Some folk thought they saw a phantom, not real, and they fell silent.

POET 3: Then Arthur—who never was afraid—saluted the stranger properly.

ARTHUR 1: Sir, welcome to this place. I am Arthur and head of this house. I pray thee, dismount, and stay here with us.

GR.KNIGHT 1: Nay, sir, to dwell for any time in this house is not my cause.

GR.KNIGHT 2: But because of thy chivalry, and that thy men are held to be the worthiest, the bravest, the most valiant, and courteous—

GR.KNIGHT 1: It is all this that has enticed me hither.

GR.KNIGHT 2: And thou may be sure by this branch of holly that I pass in peace.

GR.KNIGHT 1: But if thou be so bold as all men tell, thou wilt grant the game I ask.

NARRATOR 2: This giant wants a game? Is he fooling?

NARRATOR 1: Not on your life—so to speak.

GR.KNIGHT 2: It is now Christmastime, and I see around me many who are brave. If any in this house be so bold and daring as to strike one stroke in exchange for another, I shall give him this axe—to keep or not.

GR.KNIGHT 3: I shall take the first blow of the axe—provided I deal him another in return—after twelve months and a day.

NARRATOR 2: Hold on. Am I understanding this? This is a game—with an axe?

NARRATOR 1: Look. Pretend I have an axe—a big one, a battle-ax. You get to strike me with the axe, then you keep it—until we meet again—in this case, after a year and a day. Then it's my turn to strike you with the axe.

NARRATOR 2: And this is a game?

NARRATOR 1: Well, yes. It's a game of courage—of strength. It's a challenge!

POET 1: At first, the knight astounded everyone. Now, fear held them silent.

POET 2: The knight, righting himself in his saddle, rolled his red eyes fiercely. He bristled his bright green eyebrows and stroked his beard, waiting.

POET 3: When no one answered his challenge, he coughed—ready to speak.

GR.KNIGHT 3: (*Laughs*) What! Is this Arthur's house—this the Round Table of renown—where now all tremble without a blow being struck?

ARTHUR: (*Angry*) I know no man who fears thy great words. Give me thy axe. I will grant thee thy request!

POET 1: The king seized the axe and whirled it about, ready to strike.

From *Readers Theatre for Middle School Boys: Investigating the Strange and Mysterious* by Ann N. Black. Westport, CT: Teacher Ideas Press. Copyright © 2008.

POET 2: The Green Knight looked grim. He stroked his beard and drew down his coat and waited for the blow.

POET 3: Then Sir Gawain, sitting next to Queen Guinevere, turned to the king.

GAWAIN 1: I beseech you, sir, let me undertake this encounter.

GAWAIN 2: It is not meet, my lord, that thou should undertake this matter with so many bold ones here on the bench. My life would be the lesser loss.

GAWAIN 1: Give the game to me. It belongs not to thee.

POET 1: The noble knights all took counsel and gave the same advice—free the king and give the game to Gawain.

POET 2: The king, then, gave up the axe to Gawain and blessed him.

ARTHUR 1: Take care, cousin. Keep heart and hand steady. Make thy cut properly, for I am sure thou will endure his blow to thee later.

POET 1: Gawain then, with axe in hand, went boldly to the man in green.

GR.KNIGHT 1: Before we begin, sir knight, let us say again our agreement and tell me, as well, what thy name is.

GAWAIN 1: Gawain I am called—I, who will strike you this blow and who will receive one in return, with whatever weapon thou wilt, in twelve months and one day.

GR.KNIGHT 2: It pleases me well that thou hast truly rehearsed our terms, but thou shalt first pledge me thy word that thou will seek me thyself.

GAWAIN 2: Where shall I find thee? I know not thee—nor thy court, where thou dwellest, nor thy name. Tell me thy name and abode. I shall find thee.

GAWAIN 3: That I swear thee for truth.

GR.KNIGHT 3: When thou have struck me soundly, then will I teach thee of my house and name. (*Pause*) If I speak not, so much the better for thee. Then, thou mayest remain in thy own land and seek no further.

GR.KNIGHT 1: But now—cease thy talking! Take now thy grim tool, and let us see how thou can use it.

GAWAIN 1: Gladly, sir. Gladly.

NARRATOR 2: I can't believe this is happening—this so-called game!

NARRATOR 1: The Green Knight has thrown out the challenge. Watch Sir Gawain!

POET 1: The Green Knight knelt on the ground. He bent his head slightly and swept his long hair atop his crown, baring his neck for the blow.

POET 2: Gawain grips the axe. He raises it on high—sets his left foot forward, and—lets the axe fall quickly upon the naked flesh.

SOUND: (*Sound as if cutting an apple in two. Then a thud on the floor.*)

POET 1: The sharp blade severed the head from the body, cutting through the giant's bones, slicing, until the bright steel hit the ground.

POET 3: The fair head fell from the neck to the earth.

POET 1: Many who were watching, kicked it to one side as it rolled forth.

POET 2: Blood burst from the body and glistened on the green. Yet the knight never faltered nor fell—but boldly he strode forth. Then he stopped.

POET 1: He reached down, seized his head, and lifted it up quickly. Holding it by the hair, he turned to his horse, caught the bridle, and stepped into his stirrup. Then, though headless, he sat tall in his saddle, as if no mishap had harmed him.

From *Readers Theatre for Middle School Boys: Investigating the Strange and Mysterious* by Ann N. Black. Westport, CT: Teacher Ideas Press. Copyright © 2008.

POET 3: Turning his ugly trunk about—that ugly, bleeding body—he directed the face toward the nobles. The head lifted up its eyelids, and it spoke.

GR.KNIGHT 3: Gawain—go as thou hast promised. Seek till thou find me, according to thy promise made in this hall. Get thee to the Green Chapel.

GR.KNIGHT 2: Go, there, I charge thee, to receive, on New Year's morn, such a blow as thou hast dealt to me. As Knight of the Green Chapel, I am known to many. If thou seekest, thou cannot fail to find me.

GR.KNIGHT 1: Therefore—come (*Pause*), or coward thou will be named.

SOUND: (*Horse gallops*)

POET 1: With a fierce cry, the Green Knight turned his horse and rushed from the hall—his head in his hands, fire flying from his horse's hooves.

NARRATOR 2: And where was he flying to?

NARRATOR 1: Do you mean what land? What place? No one knew.

POET 2: King Arthur and Gawain laughed as the Green Knight rode away, but the king, in his heart, wondered much at this marvel. Yet, he let no one see he was troubled and spoke thus to his queen:

ARTHUR 1: Dear lady, be not dismayed. Such tricks as entertainment often happen at Christmastime. Indeed, I can proceed to eat my meal now, for I cannot deny I have witnessed a wondrous adventure today.

ARTHUR 2: Now, Sir Gawain, hang up thine axe, for it has hewn enough.

POET 3: So the weapon was hung above the dais that all men might look upon it and tell others the wonder of it.

POET 2: Then all the knights hastened to their seats at the table—so did the king and our good knight—and all feasted until the day was done.

 From *Readers Theatre for Middle School Boys: Investigating the Strange and Mysterious* by Ann N. Black. Westport, CT: Teacher Ideas Press. Copyright © 2008.

POET 1: A year passes full quickly and never returns. The beginning is seldom like the end.

POET 3: This Christmas passed away, and the year after it, with each season in turn following another. Thus winter winds round again, and Gawain prepares to leave on the dreaded journey he promised.

POET 2: On All-hallows Day, King Arthur entertains his court in honor of his nephew, Gawain. The company grieves over his looming departure, but they speak only of mirth. The knight, too, keeps of good cheer.

GAWAIN 1: Should I shrink from a dreaded destiny? What can a man do but try?

POET 3: On the morrow, Sir Gawain, with great ceremony, is dressed in his armor and completely equipped. He hears mass, takes leave of Arthur and the knights. All the court kiss him and commend him to Christ.

POET 1: He bids them all farewell—as he thinks—forever.

POET 2: By this time, his steed, Gringolet, was ready—his saddle shining with gold fringe and rich gold nails that glittered like gleams of the sun.

POET 3: Then, he who was never found wanting, received his shield of brilliant red with the five-pointed pentangle painted in pure gold.

POET 1: Seizing his lance, he spurs his horse, and begins his journey alone through England, always enquiring after the Green Knight of the Green Chapel, but no one has ever seen any such man of green.

POET 2: The knight pursues his journey by strange paths, encountering not only serpents, wolves, bulls, and bears, but wood satyrs and giants.

POET 3: But worse than all was the sharp winter—when the cold, clear water shed from the clouds and froze as it fell to earth.

From *Readers Theatre for Middle School Boys: Investigating the Strange and Mysterious* by Ann N. Black. Westport, CT: Teacher Ideas Press. Copyright © 2008.

POET 1: In peril and plight the knight travels on, beseeching the Virgin Mary on Christmas Eve to guide him to a place where he may hear mass.

POET 2: Scarcely has he blessed himself thrice when he sees a dwelling in the forest—a beautiful castle.

POET 3: He urges on his steed, Gringolet, but at the chief gate, he finds the drawbridge raised and the gates shut. He calls out. A porter answers.

PORTER: Who is it that calls? And what is your errand here?

GAWAIN 1: Good sir, to ask the high lord of this house to grant me a lodging.

PORTER: Yea, by Peter! Thou art welcome to dwell here as long as thou likest.

POET 3: The drawbridge is let down and the gate opened wide to receive him. His horse is well-stabled, and knights and squires bring Gawain into the hall. Then the lord of the country, his host, bids him welcome.

POET 2: Sir Gawain looks at his host. Big and bold, he seemed—a huge warrior. His face, fierce as fire, held a full beard, beaver-hued.

POET 1: Servants conduct our knight to a lavish chamber where they give him rich robes to wear. With the lords and ladies, he partakes of a full noble feast. And much mirth he makes, for the wine is in his head.

POET 2: After dinner, the company go to the chapel to hear the Christmas service. The host of the castle and Sir Gawain sit together. Then the lord's wife, accompanied by her maids, leaves her seat to join them.

GAWAIN 1: This lady appeared more fair than Guinevere. An older lady (ancient she seemed) led the lady by the hand, and very unlike were these two.

From *Readers Theatre for Middle School Boys: Investigating the Strange and Mysterious* by Ann N. Black. Westport, CT: Teacher Ideas Press. Copyright © 2008.

GAWAIN 2: If the young one was fair, the other was yellow and had rough and wrinkled cheeks.

GAWAIN 1: The younger had breast and throat displayed.

GAWAIN 2: The ancient one exposed only her black brows, her two eyes, her nose, and her naked lips, all sour and bleared. Her body was short and thick; her buttocks broad and round.

POET 1: With permission of the lord, Sir Gawain bows to the elder woman, but the younger he kisses and begs to be her servant.

POET 2: Great is the joy in the castle for three days, but at the end of the Christmas festival, Sir Gawain desires to leave. Protesting his departure, his host persuades him to stay—promising to direct him to the Green Chapel, about two miles away, for his appointed time.

GR.KNIGHT 1: Let us make an agreement then. I shall rise early to hunt. Thou shouldst lie abed at thy ease and rise at the usual hour. In the evening, we shall sit at table with my lady and exchange with each other what we have obtained during that day.

GR.KNIGHT 2: Whatever I win from the hunt shall be yours, and whatever thou gettest here in the castle shall be mine.

POET 1: And thus begins three days of hunting by the lord—and three days of his lady tempting and teasing Sir Gawain.

POET 2: This beauteous lady, each day, visited Sir Gawain in his bedchambers.

POET 3: Thus, at the end of the first day, Sir Gawain paid the lord the one kiss.

NARRATOR 1: Which we know he got from the lady.

NARRATOR 2: Wait! Doesn't the lord want to know where Gawain got that kiss?

NARRATOR 1: Maybe, but Sir Gawain tells him, "That was not in our agreement."

POET 2: The host laughs and pays his bounty—flesh from a deer fresh dressed.

POET 3: Second day—the same. The lady visits Sir Gawain in his bedchamber. She teases and tempts him again. So—he pays two kisses that night.

POET 1: The lord has hunted wild swine all day. He returns with his trophy, the bloody head of a boar mounted on a pole, and gives it to Gawain.

POET 1: On the third day, the lady coaxes even more. She asks the reluctant Gawain for a gift to remember him by. But he has nothing to give.

LADY: Though I have nought of yours, ye should have something of mine.

POET 1: And she offers him a rich ring of red gold—but he refuses the ring, as he has nothing to give her in return.

POET 2: The lady then loosens her bright cloak to reveal a belt of green silk, fringed and embroidered with gold.

LADY: Since ye refuse my ring because it seems too rich, and ye would not be beholden to me, I shall give you this belt that is less valuable.

POET 3: But again Sir Gawain refuses.

LADY: Do ye refuse it because it seems simple and of little value? (*Secretly*) Hark! There are powers knit within it—for he who is girded with this green lace cannot be wounded or slain by any man under heaven.

POET 3: With this, he accepts the lace, and promises to keep it well hidden.

POET 1: Night falls. The host presents Gawain with a skin—stripped from the fox he killed and ripped from the mouths of his hounds.

POET 2: Gawain forfeits his three kisses from the lady—but giving them to his host, he shows not nor tells not of the green belt.

POET 1: At last, New Year's Day approaches. Sir Gawain declares that, in the morning, he must leave for the Green Chapel and his appointment. He asks his host for a man to guide him there. But on the morrow—

POET 3: The weather is stormy. Snow falls. The hills are full of drifts.

POET 1: But Sir Gawain clothed himself in his rich weeds and his armour—not forgetting the belt of green lace, the lady's gift.

POET 2: Ready now, he calls for his steed.

POET 1: The bridge is down, the gates open. The knight, with his guide, goes forward to that place where he shall receive the dreaded blow.

POET 3: The second day, after climbing over cliffs and up and down the hills, they reach a high hill covered with snow.

GUIDE 1: Master, I have brought thee hither at this time. Ye are not far from that noted place that ye have so often enquired after. The place is esteemed full perilous—and the man who dwells in that wasteland is the worst upon earth. He is stiff and stern and loves to strike.

GUIDE 2: Greater is he than any man upon middle-earth. His body is bigger than the best four in King Arthur's house.

GUIDE 1: It is he who keeps the Green Chapel. None passes by that place that he doesn't strike them to death with a mere swipe of his hand. I tell ye truly, ye come there, ye be killed.

GUIDE 2: Aye. Good Sir Gawain, for God's sake, go to some other country.

From *Readers Theatre for Middle School Boys: Investigating the Strange and Mysterious* by Ann N. Black. Westport, CT: Teacher Ideas Press. Copyright © 2008.

GAWAIN 1: I thank thee for thy well-meant kindness, but though the owner of the Chapel be a stern knave, I must go there.

GUIDE 1: Mary! Since it pleases thee to lose thy life, I will not hinder thee. (*Sighs*) Have thy helmet on thy head, thy spear in thy hand, and ride down this path by yon rockslide, till thou be brought to the bottom of the valley. Then look a little on the plain, on thy left hand, and thou shalt see the chapel itself and the burly knight that guards it.

GUIDE 2: Farewell, Gawain, the noble! For all the gold upon ground I would not go with thee through this wood one foot farther.

POET 1: Gawain continues on his journey, rides through the dale, and looks about. The very shadows of the woods seem wild and distorted, but no chapel can he see—until he investigates a strange, rocky crag—and he hears a wondrous wild noise.

SOUND: (*Harsh grating sound of rock upon rock*)

GAWAIN 1: Who dwells in this place? What discourse with me to hold?

GR.KNIGHT 1: Stay! Abide! Thou shalt have all in haste that which I promised thee.

POET 2: Out of a hole in the crag, came the knight in green carrying a new axe.

GR.KNIGHT 1: Gawain! Truly thou art welcome to my place. Thou hast timed thy travel, as a true man should. Thou knowest the covenant between us, that on New Year's Day I should return thy blow.

GR.KNIGHT 2: Have, therefore, thy helmet off thy head, and take thy pay at once.

GAWAIN 1: By God, I shall not begrudge thee thy will.

POET 3: Then Sir Gawain shows his bare neck—and appears undaunted.

From *Readers Theatre for Middle School Boys: Investigating the Strange and Mysterious* by Ann N. Black. Westport, CT: Teacher Ideas Press. Copyright © 2008.

POET 2: The man in green seizes his grim tool.

NARRATOR 2: (*Loud whisper*) The axe! The axe!

NARRATOR 1: Aye. But a different axe—a new one.

POET 2: With all his force, the man in green raises aloft the shiny axe.

POET 1: The axe comes gliding down, down. Sir Gawain shrinks a little with his shoulders. (*Pause*) The knight in green withholds the weapon!

GR.KNIGHT 1: Ha! Thou art not Gawain who is so high esteemed. Thou fleest from fear before thou feelest harm. Such cowardice I never did hear.

GR.KNIGHT 2: I never flinched when thou struck. My head flew to my feet, yet I never fled. I deserve to be called the better man!

GAWAIN 1: I flinched once, but will do so no more, though my head fall on the stones. But hasten! Deal me my destiny!

GR.KNIGHT 2: Have at thee, then!

POET 1: The man in green heaves the axe aloft again and looks as savagely as if he were mad. He aims at Gawain—but stops—withholds his hand.

GR.KNIGHT 1: Since now thou hast thy heart whole, it behooves me to strike—so take care of thy neck!

GAWAIN 2: Thrash on! Thou threatenest too long. I believe thy own heart fails.

GR.KNIGHT 2: Forsooth! Since thou speakest so boldly, I will no longer delay!

POET 2: He lets fall his axe on the bare neck of Sir Gawain. The sharp weapon cuts into the flesh. Blood spurts—shoots out bright red.

POET 3: When Sir Gawain sees his blood on the snow, he draws out his sword.

From *Readers Theatre for Middle School Boys: Investigating the Strange and Mysterious* by Ann N. Black. Westport, CT: Teacher Ideas Press. Copyright © 2008.

GAWAIN 1: Cease, man! Cease! Our agreement stipulates only one stroke.

GR.KNIGHT 1: Bold knight, be not so wroth. I promised thee a stroke, and thou hast it. Two blows I aimed at thee, for twice thou kissed my fair wife, but thou restorest the kisses to me according to agreement. The third time, thou failed—for that girdle, given thee by my wife, belongs to me.

GR.KNIGHT 2: I know well thy conduct—for it was I who sent my wife to try thee. Thou had seemest the fair knight who was the most faultless—in good faith, prized more highly than other gallant knights.

GR.KNIGHT 3: But sir, thou lacked a little in loyalty—not for the wooing of my wife and not for wickedness, but because you loved your own life. Ah, but for this, I blame thee less.

POET 1: Gawain, listening to the sharp words, stood confounded with grief and self-disgust. He shrank within for shame. Blood rushed to his face.

NARRATOR 2: Oh. He wanted the green belt to save him. He was afraid! Now, what?

POET 2: He unties the green belt. Fiercely, he flings it at the feet of the knight.

GAWAIN 1: There lies vileness and vice—and virtue destroyed! Cursed be all coveting! Cursed be cowardice!

GAWAIN 2: It was fear of thy blow, knight. It was that cowardice that brought me to coveting. I am faulty and false—I, who ever feared disloyalty and lies. Let me gain thy grace anew, sir. Hereafter, I shall keep watch.

GR.KNIGHT 1: (*Laughs*) Thou art confessed so clean, that I hold thee as pure as if thou hadst never been guilty. I give to thee, sir, the gold-fringed girdle as a token of thy adventure at the Green Chapel. But come, again, sir, to my castle.

GAWAIN 1: Nay, forsooth. Methinks I should be excused. But the girdle—I will wear it in remembrance of my faults. (*Pause*) Only, tell me your right name and I shall be off.

GR.KNIGHT: I am Bernlak de Hautdesert, acting by the cunning of Morgan le Fay, Merlin's pupil. She was the ancient lady whom you met—who sent me to test the fame of the Round Table. But do come to the castle, sir.

POET 2: Gawain refuses, and riding Gringolet full fair, he returns to King Arthur's hall to relate his adventures, to reveal his shame, and to recount the symbol of the green belt he wears.

POET 1: The king and his courtiers comfort the knight, and all agree they should ever after wear a bright, green belt for Gawain's sake.

NARRATOR 1: Thus—in King Arthur's time this adventure befell.

NARRATOR 2: Sir Gawain and the Green Knight—a wonderful story to tell!

From *Readers Theatre for Middle School Boys: Investigating the Strange and Mysterious* by Ann N. Black. Westport, CT: Teacher Ideas Press. Copyright © 2008.

Twisting the Tale with O. Henry

Welcome to a wild adventure told by the inimitable O. Henry, the storyteller of one intriguing yarn after the other whose friends and colleagues, eight years after his death, established our nation's most prestigious award for short fiction—the man who, like the characters in his stories, lived a life of surprising twists and turns.

He was born William Sidney Porter in Greensboro, North Carolina, in 1862. As a teenager, he became a licens_____ st, but ill health and a desire to see the West led him to Texas where he _____ k, clerk, cartoonist, guitarist, and singer. Then in 1887, he eloped with _____ their daughter was born.

_____ g maps for the General Land Office in Austin, Porter was always writ-_____ unded an ill-fated comic magazine, *The Rolling Stone.* But his map job _____ nk accountant. However, when shortages in his accounts appeared, he _____ embezzlement, but the family moved to Houston where he became a _____ . Soon, however, he left the country and did not return until his wife's _____ Indicted, he faced the five-year prison sentence he had tried to avoid. _____ years in the penitentiary, ironically serving as the night-duty phar-_____ ite, honing the style that would make him famous but under his new, _____ ry. Once released, and after reuniting with his daughter and marry-_____ ved to New York.

_____ dred short stories published, success was his. Unfortunately, con-_____ g dissipation took its toll, and William Sidney Porter (O. Henry) _____ ears old.

PRODUCTION NOTES

The humorist and journalist, O. Henry, born William Sidney Porter, continues to receive honors almost a hundred years after his death. In Austin, Texas, where he lived and worked, a middle school carries his name, and the city sponsors an O. Henry Museum, as well. The original O. Henry Memorial Award of 1918, which was intended to "strengthen the art of the short story and to stimulate younger authors," has now burgeoned into a new category: The O. Henry Awards for prize-winning short stories written by young people were announced in 2006.

"The Ransom of Red Chief," O. Henry's ironic spoof of a kidnapping, amuses both the young and the old, but it surely speaks to young boys. Often O. Henry's unusual terms and spellings add even more spice to the story. The following Readers Theatre adaptation calls for fourteen students: eleven readers and three sound-effects people. The script can be cast exclusively with boys. If, however, girls are to be included, Readers 3 and 5, in particular, were written with that possibility in mind.

Sound effects are suggested throughout the script. The Sound Appendix gives suggestions for each specific effect. However, the boys in the cast will no doubt invent their own strategies to create the sounds. Sound effects can be struck from the script without any real loss.

Fifteen scripts with black folders are needed (eleven for the cast, three for Sounds A, B, and C, and one for the teacher).

Fourteen reading stands can be used, if desired (for the cast and Sounds A, B, and C).

Twisting the Tale with O. Henry (William Sidney Porter)

"The Ransom of Red Chief"

	Sounds A	B	C	
	X	X	X	
Dorsets 6, 7		Readers 1–5		Johnny
X X		X X X X X		X
	Sam		Bill	
	X		X	

READERS 3, 5: (*Low laughter, as at a private joke*)

READER 2: I do not see what is so funny!

READER 4: Me neither. This is an <u>ug</u>-ly story.

READER 5: (*Mock shudders*) Ohhhh. You're scared!

READER 2: No way! A story by O. Henry? He writes funny stuff. (*Pause*) Well, this is a funny story, but it's about—the Dark Side—about Crime!

READER 4: You're right. It's about a kidnapping gone bad. You've heard the saying *The love of money is the root of all evil*?

READERS 3, 5: Yes, of course.

READER 4: Good. And you've heard another one that *Crime doesn't pay*?

SOUND A: (*Sound of coins dropping slowly*)

READER 3: Of course we have! Even O. Henry found that out for himself.

READER 5: He sure did! A bank said he stole money. He went to prison for that.

READER 2: But O. Henry was no ordinary criminal. He was a respectable family man—and already a writer. And he kept on writing, even in prison.

READER 4: And becoming famous, even in prison, he dropped his real name, William Sidney Porter, and became the author we know—O. Henry.

READER 5: So, what if he's been famous. Kidnapping is funny? No. It's a crime!

SOUND A: (*Sound of coins more insistent*)

READER 4: Sure! But O. Henry twists that around in The Ransom of Red Chief.

READER 1: Which we will now present for you. Gather up that money!

SOUND A: (*Coins gathered into bag or box*)

READER 1: Very good. Gentlemen, let's begin!

BILL: It looked like a good thing.

From *Readers Theatre for Middle School Boys: Investigating the Strange and Mysterious* by Ann N. Black. Westport, CT: Teacher Ideas Press. Copyright © 2008.

READER 1: But wait till I tell you.

SAM: We were down South, in Alabama—Bill Driscoll and myself—when this kidnapping idea struck us. There was a town down there, as flat as a flannel-cake and called Summit—of course.

READER 2: Of course. Summit—the top of a hill, but flat as a pancake!

SAM: Bill and me had a joint capital of about six hundred dollars.

SOUND A: (*Noise of coins jingling*)

BILL: And we needed just two thousand dollars more to pull off a fraudulent town-lot scheme in Western Illinois.

SOUND A: (*Coins thump and are quiet*)

BILL: Phi-lo-pro-gen-i-tive-ness, says we, is strong in semi-rural communities, and a kidnapping project ought to do better there.

READER 3: A kidnapping project? Based on some fancy word?

READER 4: This scheme is going to work because these simple people in Summit love their kids!

READER 5: But what about the police? They'll be on the trail in no time!

SAM: (*Grinning*) Summit couldn't get after us with anything stronger than constables, and, maybe, some lackadaisical bloodhounds.

BILL: So, it looked good. We selected for our victim the only child of a prominent citizen named Ebenezer Dorset.

SAM: The father was respectable and tight, a mortgage fancier—

SOUND A: (*A few coins drop after* mortgage fancier)

From *Readers Theatre for Middle School Boys: Investigating the Strange and Mysterious* by Ann N. Black. Westport, CT: Teacher Ideas Press. Copyright © 2008.

BILL: And a stern, upright collection-plate passer and forecloser.

SOUND A: (*More coins drop*)

SAM: The kid was a boy of about ten with freckles—and hair the color of the cover of a magazine you buy at a news-stand when you want to catch a train. Bill and me figured that Ebenezer would melt down for a ransom of two thousand dollars to a cent.

READER 3: That sounds like some scheme!

SAM: But wait till I tell you. About two miles from Summit was a little mountain, covered with a dense cedar brake. On the rear elevation of this mountain was a cave. There we stored our provisions.

BILL: One evening, we drove in a buggy past old Dorset's house.

SOUND C: (*Sound of horse on dirt road during next line*)

SAM: The kid was in the street, throwing rocks at a kitten.

SOUND B: (*Two angry cat snarls*)

BILL: Hey, little boy! Would you like to have some candy and a nice ride?

SAM: The boy catches Bill neatly in the eye with a piece of brick.

BILL: (*Angry*) That will cost the old man an extra five hundred dollars!

READER 4: That boy put up a fight like a welterweight cinnamon bear.

SAM: But at last we got him down in the buggy and drove up to the cave.

SOUND C: (*Horse on dirt road*)

SAM (continues): Then I hitched the horse in the cedar brake.

SOUND B: (*Brief horse whinny*)

From *Readers Theatre for Middle School Boys: Investigating the Strange and Mysterious* by Ann N. Black. Westport, CT: Teacher Ideas Press. Copyright © 2008.

SAM (continues): After dark I drove the buggy to the little village, where we had hired it, and walked back to the mountain.

READER 4: A fire was burning behind the big rock at the entrance of the cave.

READER 2: And the boy was watching a pot of boiling coffee with two buzzard tail-feathers stuck in his red hair.

SAM: He points a stick at me when I come up.

JOHNNY: Ha! Cursed paleface, do you dare to enter the camp of Red Chief, the terror of the plains?

READER 2: Bill rolled up his trouser and examined some bruises on his shins.

BILL: He's all right now. We're playing Indian. I'm Old Hank, the Trapper, Red Chief's captive, and I'm going to be scalped at daybreak. By Geronimo! That kid can kick hard!

READER 1: Yes, sir, that boy seemed to be having the time of his life. The fun of camping out in a cave had made him forget that he was a captive, too.

SAM: He christened me Snake-eye, the Spy. Then he announced that when his braves returned from the warpath, I was to be broiled at the stake at the rising of the sun. (*Pause*) Then we had supper.

READER 1: He filled his mouth full of bacon and bread and gravy, and began to talk. He made a during-dinner speech something like this:

JOHNNY: I like this fine. I never camped out before; but I had a pet possum once, and I was nine last birthday. I hate to go to school.

SAM: (*Small laughter*) And—are there any real Indians in these woods?

JOHNNY: I want some more gravy. Does the trees moving make the wind blow? What makes your nose so red, Hank? My father has lots of money.

BILL: *(Patiently)* And—are the stars hot? Why are oranges round?

JOHNNY: Have you got beds to sleep on in this cave? A parrot can talk, but a monkey or a fish can't. How many does it take to make twelve?

READER 2: Every few minutes he would tiptoe to the mouth of the cave to rubber for the scouts of the hated paleface.

READER 4: Now and then he would let out a war-whoop that made Old Hank the Trapper shiver.

READER 1: Yes, sir. That boy had Bill terrorized from the start.

SAM: "Red Chief," says I to the kid, "would you like to go home?"

JOHNNY: Aw, I don't have any fun at home. I hate to go to school. I like to camp out. You won't take me back home again, Snake-eye, will you?

SAM: Not right away. We'll stay here in the cave a while.

JOHNNY: All right! That'll be fine. I never had such fun in all my life.

SAM: We went to bed about eleven o'clock.

BILL: He kept us awake for three hours, jumping up and reaching for his stick rifle and screeching, "Hist! Pard!"

READER 1: The fancied crackle of a twig or the rustle of a leaf revealed to his young imagination the stealthy approach of a band of outlaws.

SAM: At last, I fell into a troubled sleep, and dreamed I had been kidnapped and chained to a tree by a ferocious pirate with red hair. At daybreak, I awoke to an awful series of screams from Bill. It's an awful thing to hear a strong, desperate, fat man scream in a cave at daybreak.

From *Readers Theatre for Middle School Boys: Investigating the Strange and Mysterious* by Ann N. Black. Westport, CT: Teacher Ideas Press. Copyright © 2008.

READER 1: Red Chief was sitting on Bill's chest, with one hand twined in Bill's hair. In the other, he had the sharp knife we used for slicing bacon.

READER 4: He was industriously and realistically trying to take Bill's scalp.

SAM: I got the knife away from the kid, but from that moment, Bill's spirit was broken.

READER 2: He lay down on his side of the bed, but he never closed an eye again in sleep as long as that boy was there.

SAM: I dozed off, but about sun-up I remembered that Red Chief had said I was to be burned at the stake at the rising of the sun. I wasn't nervous or afraid; but I sat up and lit my pipe and leaned against a rock.

BILL: What you getting up so soon for, Sam?

SAM: Me? Oh, I got a kind of a pain in my shoulder. I thought sitting up would rest it.

BILL: You're a liar! You're afraid. You was to be burned at sunrise, and you was afraid he'd do it. And he would, too, if he could find a match. *(Pause)* Ain't it awful, Sam? Do you think anybody will pay out money to get a little imp like that back home?

SAM: Sure. A rowdy kid like that is just the kind that parents dote on. Now, you and the Chief get up and cook breakfast, while I go reconnoiter.

READER 4: Over by Summit, Sam expected to see the sturdy yeomanry of the village beating the countryside for the dastardly kidnappers.

READER 2: Instead, he saw a peaceful landscape dotted with one man ploughing.

READER 4: Nobody was dragging the creek; no couriers dashed hither and yon, bringing tidings of no news to the distracted parents.

SAM: So I went down the mountain to breakfast. When I got to the cave, I found Bill backed up against the side of it, breathing hard.

READER 4: The boy was threatening to smash him with a rock half as big as a coconut. Bill tried to explain what had happened.

BILL: He put a red-hot boiled potato down my back—and then mashed it with his foot; and I boxed his ears. (*Slight pause*) Have you got a gun about you, Sam?

JOHNNY: I'll fix you! No man ever yet struck the Red Chief but what he got paid for it. You better beware!

READER 4: After breakfast the kid takes a piece of leather with strings wrapped around it out of his pocket and goes outside the cave unwinding it.

BILL: What's he up to now? You don't think he'll run away, do you, Sam?

SAM: No fear of it. He don't seem to be much of a homebody, and there don't seem to be much excitement around Summit on account of his disappearance. Anyhow, he'll be missed today. Tonight we must get a message to his father demanding two thousand dollars for his return.

READER 1: Just then—a kind of war-whoop! It was a sling that Red Chief had pulled out of his pocket, and he was whirling it around his head.

SAM: I dodged—and heard a heavy thud and a kind of sigh from Bill, like a horse gives out when you take his saddle off.

READER 2: A rock the size of an egg had caught Bill just behind his left ear.

READER 4: He loosened himself all over and fell in the fire across the frying pan of hot water for washing dishes.

SOUND C: (*A thud. Metal pan falls against wood.*)

SOUND A: (*A splash of water*)

READER 1: By and by, Bill sits up and feels behind his ear.

SAM: Take it easy—you'll come to your senses presently.

BILL: You won't go away and leave me here alone, will you, Sam?

SAM: I went out and caught that boy and shook him until his freckles rattled. "If you don't behave," says I, "I'll take you straight home. Now, are you going to be good, or not?"

JOHNNY: I was only funning. I didn't mean to hurt Old Hank. But what did he hit me for? I'll behave, Snake-eye, if you won't send me home—and if you'll let me play the Black Scout today.

SAM: That's for you and Mr. Bill to decide. He's your playmate for the day. I'm going away for a while on business. Now, you come in and make friends with him and say you are sorry for hurting him, or home you go, at once. (*Pause*) I made him and Bill shake hands. Then I told Bill we had to send a letter to old man Dorset that day, demanding the ransom and how it should be paid.

BILL: You know, Sam, I've stood by you without batting an eye in earthquakes, fire and flood—in poker games, dynamite outrages, police raids, train robberies and cyclones. I never lost my nerve yet—till we kidnapped that two-legged skyrocket of a kid. He's got me going. You won't leave me long with him, will you, Sam?

SAM: You must keep the boy amused and quiet.

READER 1: Bill and Sam got paper and pencil and worked on the letter to old Dorset, while Red Chief, with a blanket wrapped around him, strutted up and down, guarding the mouth of the cave.

BILL: (*Pleading, tearfully*) Make the ransom fifteen hundred dollars instead of two thousand. I ain't attempting to decry the celebrated and moral aspect of parental affection, but we're dealing with humans, and it ain't human for anybody to give up two thousand dollars for that forty-pound chunk of freckled wildcat. I'm willing to take a chance at fifteen hundred dollars. You can charge the difference up to me.

SAM: So, to relieve Bill, I acceded, and we collaborated on a letter that ran this way:

READER 3: Ebenezer Dorset, Esquire:

READER 5: We have your boy concealed in a place far from Summit. It is useless for you or the most skilful detectives to attempt to find him. The only terms on which you can have him restored to you are these:

READER 3: We demand fifteen hundred dollars in large bills for his return: the money to be left at midnight tonight at the same spot and in the same box as your reply—as hereinafter described.

READER 5: If you agree to these terms, send your answer in writing by a solitary messenger tonight at half-past eight o'clock.

READER 3: After crossing Owl Creek, on the road to Poplar Cove, there are three large trees about a hundred yards apart, close to the fence of the wheat field on the right-hand side. At the bottom of the fence-post, opposite the third tree, will be found a small pasteboard box.

READER 5: The messenger will place the answer in this box and return immediately to Summit.

READER 3: If you attempt any treachery or fail to comply with our demand as stated (*Slowly, threateningly*), you will never see your boy again.

 From *Readers Theatre for Middle School Boys: Investigating the Strange and Mysterious* by Ann N. Black. Westport, CT: Teacher Ideas Press. Copyright © 2008.

READER 5: If you pay the money as demanded, he will be returned to you safe and well within three hours.

SAM: These terms are final, and if you do not accede to them no further communication will be attempted.

READER 1: And the letter to Red Chief's father is signed, Two Desperate Men.

SAM: I addressed the envelope to Dorset, and put it in my pocket. As I was about to leave, the kid comes up to me.

JOHNNY: Aw, Snake-eye, you said I could play the Black Scout today.

SAM: Of course. Mr. Bill will play with you. What kind of game is it?

JOHNNY: I'm the Black Scout, and I have to ride to the stockade to warn the settlers that the Indians are coming. I'm tired of playing Indian by myself. I want to be the Black Scout.

SAM: All right. It sounds harmless to me. I guess Mr. Bill will help you foil the pesky savages.

BILL: (*Suspiciously*) What am I to do?

JOHNNY: You are the hoss. Get down on your hands and knees. How can I ride to the stockade without a hoss?

READER 2: Bill gets down on his all fours, and a look comes in his eye like a rabbit's when you catch it in a trap.

BILL: (*Still suspicious*) How far is it to the stockade, kid?

JOHNNY: Ninety miles. You have to hump it to get there on time. Whoa, now!

READER 4: The Black Scout jumps on Bill's back and digs his heels in his side.

BILL: For Heaven's sake, hurry back, Sam, as soon as you can. I wish we hadn't made the ransom more than a thousand. (*Pause. Short yelp.*) Say, you quit kicking me, or I'll get up and warm you good!

SAM: I walked over to Poplar Cove and posted my letter. When I got back to the cave, Bill and the boy were not to be found. So I lighted my pipe and sat down on a mossy bank to await developments. In about half an hour I heard the bushes rustle.

READER 1: Bill wobbled out into the little glade in front of the cave.

READER 2: (*Loud whisper*) Behind him was the kid, (*Slowly*) stepping softly like a scout—with a broad grin on his face.

READER 4: Bill took off his hat, and wiped his face with a red handkerchief.

READER 2: (*Loud whisper again*) The kid stopped about eight feet behind him.

BILL: Sam, I suppose you'll think I'm a renegade, but I couldn't help it. The boy is gone. I have sent him home. All is off. I tried to be faithful, but there came a limit.

SAM: What's the trouble, Bill?

BILL: I was rode the ninety miles to the stockade, not barring an inch. Then, when the settlers was rescued, I was given oats. Sand ain't a palatable substitute. I tell you, Sam, a human being can only stand so much. (*Pause*) But he's gone—gone home. I showed him the road to Summit and kicked him about eight feet nearer there with one kick. I'm sorry we lose the ransom, but it was either that or Bill Driscoll to the madhouse.

READER 1: Bill is puffing and blowing, but there is a look of peace and growing content on his rose-pink features.

SAM: Bill, there isn't any heart disease in your family, is there?

BILL: No, nothing chronic except malaria and accidents. (*Pause*) Why?

SAM: Then you might turn around and have a look behind you.

READER 1: Bill turns and sees the boy, and loses his complexion. He sits down plump on the ground and begins to pluck aimlessly at grass and little sticks.

SAM: For an hour I was afraid of his mind. Then I told him my scheme—that we would get the ransom and be off with it by midnight if old Dorset fell in with our proposition.

READER 2: So Bill braced up enough to give the kid a weak sort of smile and a promise to play the Russian in a Japanese war with him—as soon as he felt a little better.

JOHNNY: Pow! Pow!

SAM: I had a scheme for collecting that ransom without danger of being caught.

READER 4: The tree under which the answer was to be left—and the money later on—was close to the road fence with big, bare fields on all sides.

SAM: At half-past eight I was up in that tree as well hidden as a tree toad, waiting for the messenger to arrive.

READER 1: Exactly on time, a half-grown boy rides up the road on a bicycle, locates the pasteboard box at the foot of the fence-post, slips a folded piece of paper into it and pedals away again back toward Summit.

SAM: I waited an hour and then concluded the thing was square. (*Slowly and mysteriously*) I slid down the tree, got the note, slipped along the fence till I struck the woods, and was back at the cave in another half hour. I opened the note, got near the lantern, and read it to Bill.

READER 5: It was written with a pen in a crabbed hand—addressed to Two Desperate Men:

DORSET 6: Gentlemen: I received your letter today by post, in regard to the ransom you ask for the return of my son.

DORSET 7: I think you are a little high in your demands, and I hereby make you a counter-proposition, which I am inclined to believe you will accept.

DORSET 6: You bring Johnny home and pay me two hundred and fifty dollars in cash, and I agree to take him off your hands.

DORSET 7: You had better come at night, for the neighbors believe he is lost.

DORSET 6: And I couldn't be responsible for what they would do to anybody they saw bringing him back. (*Pause*) Very respectfully, Ebenezer Dorset.

SAM: Of all the impudent—but I glanced at Bill. He had the most appealing look in his eyes I ever saw on the face of a dumb or a talking brute.

BILL: Sam, what's two hundred and fifty dollars after all? We've got the money. One more night of this kid will send me to a bed in Bedlam. Besides being a thorough gentleman, I think Mr. Dorset is a spendthrift for making us such a liberal offer. You ain't going to let the chance go, are you?

SAM: Tell you the truth, Bill, this little lamb has got on my nerves, too. We'll take him home, pay the ransom, and make our get-away.

READER 1: They took him home that night. It was just twelve o'clock when they knocked at Ebenezer's front door.

SOUND C: (*Knock on door. Pause. Repeat knock.*)

SAM: Just at the moment when I should have been abstracting the fifteen hundred dollars from the box under the tree—

SOUND A: (*Coins spill out in profusion*)

SAM: Bill was counting two hundred and fifty dollars into Dorset's hand.

READER 5: When the kid found out they were going to leave him at home, he started up a howl like a calliope.

SOUND B: *HOWL*

DORSET 7: He fastened himself as tight as a leech to Bill's leg.

READER 1: His father peeled him away gradually, like a plaster—a Band-aid.

BILL: How long can you hold him?

DORSET 6: I'm not as strong as I used to be—but I think I can promise you ten minutes.

BILL: Enough! In ten minutes I shall cross the Central, Southern, and Middle Western states, and be legging it for the Canadian border!

SAM: And, as dark as it was, and as fat as Bill was, and as good a runner as I am, he was a good mile and a half out of Summit before I could catch up with him.

READER 3: (*Pause*) Hey, you were absolutely right! This was no ordinary crime.

READER 5: Oh, we see. This was no serious crime. That little boy turned the tables on those guys.

READER 1: It's The Ransom of Red Chief—a twisted tale—by our man, our author, William Sidney Porter—known as the famous O. Henry! See for yourself. It's a great story. Read it!

Headless in "Sleepy Hollow" with Washington Irving

Washington Irving has been called "the first American writer to achieve international fame," yet today his popularity is definitely low-key. So why should we be drawn to the writings of this man? Certainly his works are more difficult to read than those of our contemporary writers. His style reflects an earlier age. His vocabulary is obviously rooted in another time. His histories have been overtaken. Some of his satires have lost their bite. Still, he was unique two hundred years ago; he remains unique today.

Born a New Yorker on April 3, 1783, Washington Irving was the eleventh child and fifth (surviving) son of parents who were well established in business, politics, and the law. In many ways, he was to emulate their successes. He worked in the family hardware business, supported Aaron Burr (who was vice president under President Thomas Jefferson), and studied law, eventually becoming the U.S. ambassador to Spain. Warmly mentored by his brothers, Washington Irving still carved his own niche in the scheme of things, eventually becoming a world-famous author, admired by his contemporaries, such as Charles Dickens and Edgar Allan Poe.

Irving began his career as a journalist of sharp commentaries when he was only nineteen. He rejected a formal higher education and, in 1806 took his first of numerous trips to England and Europe. Upon his return, Irving began to expand upon the whimsical comments and caricatures of his fellow Americans, whom he had written about earlier, especially New Yorkers. Frequently writing behind an ill-concealed literary mask such as that of Diedrich Knickerbocker, Washington Irving emerged as a true man of letters.

Known primarily today for his stories "Rip Van Winkle" and "The Legend of Sleepy Hollow," this lifelong bachelor, canny observer, and gentle humorist died at age seventy-six—a storyteller of Americana who probed beneath pretense and found our stories.

PRODUCTION NOTES

As beloved as the scrawny, superstitious Ichabod Crane is to us, his story takes some imagination on our part to read it well in performance; but, of course, discovering his all-too human qualities reflects what literature is all about. Washington Irving had a gift for sensing our foibles, and he loved to point them out to us, especially in his famous story, "The Legend of Sleepy Hollow."

Because Irving wrote this story in the guise of an imaginary storyteller, Diedrich Knickerbocker, our Readers Theatre script employs four Knickerbocker Readers to narrate major parts of the story. Two Pedagogues and two Historians also contribute to the narration. The parts of Mr. Van Tassel, Mrs. Van Tassel, Katrina, Gunpowder, and Ichabod supply additional descriptions of the storyline. The Student seeks biographical information at the opening, and he (or she) comments on the whole enterprise at the closing. All in all, the script calls for fourteen readers.

Since sounds can add much to the enjoyment of an oral reading of this story, the script calls for four students to handle the suspenseful sound effects, which range from horses plodding, galloping, and whinnying to the calls of a whippoorwill, a tree toad, a screech owl, a barking dog, a cock crow, and cricket chirps. In addition, Ichabod hears wind blowing, branches scraping, a snap of the birch rod, and his own whistling. The sound effects, of course, can be eliminated, but suggestions for developing them appear in the Sound Appendix. A *Splat* for the pumpkin might be added.

Eighteen scripts are required for the cast of fourteen and sound crew of four, plus one script for the teacher.

Headless in "Sleepy Hollow" with Washington Irving

Sounds A, B	Mr. Van T.	Katrina	Mrs. Van T.	Sounds C, D
X X	X	X	X	X X
	Gunpowder	Student		
	X	X		
Pedagogue 1	Historian 1, 2		Ichabod	Pedagogue 2
X	X X		X	X
Knickerbockers 1 & 2			Knickerbockers 3 & 4	
X X			X X	

HISTORIAN 1: Have a question for you. Do you believe in fate? (*Pause as Student shakes head*) Karma? Serendipity? How about juxtaposition?

STUDENT:	Is this a trick question? And what does it have to do with this story?
HISTORIAN 1:	Maybe a lot—maybe a little. Depends on your view of coincidence.
STUDENT:	I didn't know there was anything mysterious about this author.
HISTORIAN 1:	I don't know if there is. But check out his name—Washington Irving!
STUDENT:	So? Named after our first president—George Washington.
PEDAGOGUE 1:	Sorry. General Washington—Mr. Irving's born too early for that.
HISTORIAN 1:	How about this connection—the same month Washington Irving's born, General Washington officially proclaims peace with the British.
PEDAGOGUE 2:	Fact: That would be in 1783. End of the Revolutionary War. Coincidence? Maybe—but reason enough to be a patriot!
HISTORIAN 2:	Exactly! Reason enough for Washington Irving to celebrate America.
PEDAGOGUE 1:	True, but you know he did borrow legends from Germany, like for this story of Sleepy Hollow.
STUDENT:	So, whose story is this anyhow?
HISTORIAN 1:	Well—it's actually Diedrich Knickerbocker's story.
PEDAGOGUE 1:	Nonsense! Knickerbocker merely acts as the storyteller for Irving's legends and histories. He's just a character that Irving invented.
K'BOCKER 1:	We're invented? I don't think so!
K'BOCKER 2:	Certainly not!
K'BOCKER 3:	What an idea! Invented?
K'BOCKER 4:	I beg your pardon. Suspend your disbelief, please!

From *Readers Theatre for Middle School Boys: Investigating the Strange and Mysterious* by Ann N. Black. Westport, CT: Teacher Ideas Press. Copyright © 2008.

HISTORIAN 2: Well, at least you cannot deny this story is definitely set in America.

PEDAGOGUE 1: True again. Irving used a real place. If you go to New York City, you'll see the Hudson River on one side of the island. Travel north on that river, and you'll come to Tarrytown. Right, Mr. Knickerbocker?

K'BOCKER 1: (*Nods and begins*) Not far from this village, perhaps about two miles, there is a little valley—one of the quietest places in the whole world.

K'BOCKER 2: From the listless repose of the place, and the peculiar character of its inhabitants—descendants from the original Dutch settlers, this sequestered glen has long been known by the name of Sleepy Hollow.

K'BOCKER 3: A drowsy, dreamy influence seems to hang over the land, and to pervade the very atmosphere.

K'BOCKER 4: Some say the place was bewitched in the early days, but certain it is that some witching power still holds a spell over the good people.

K'BOCKER 1: The dominant spirit, however, that haunts this enchanted region is the apparition of a figure on horseback—without a head.

SOUND A: (*Brief soft sounds of galloping horse through the next few lines*)

PEDAGOGUE 1: It is said to be the ghost of a Hessian trooper—whose head had been carried away by a cannonball during the late war. Headless, you see.

K'BOCKER 1: The body was buried in the churchyard. Its ghost rides forth in nightly quest of his head, then hurries back to the churchyard before daylight.

PEDAGOGUE 2: Legendary superstition—the Headless Horseman of Sleepy Hollow.

K'BOCKER 1: In this by-place, there lived a worthy creature by the name of Ichabod Crane—who tarried in Sleepy Hollow for the purpose of instructing the children of that vicinity. A true pedagogue!

K'BOCKER 2: He was tall and lank, with narrow shoulders, long arms and legs, hands that dangled a mile out of his sleeves, feet that might have served for shovels—and his whole frame most loosely hung together.

K'BOCKER 1: His head was small, and flat on top—with huge ears, large green, glassy eyes, and a long snipe nose—very like a crane itself.

K'BOCKER 3: One might have mistaken him for a scarecrow eloped from a field.

ICHABOD: The schoolhouse was a low building of one large room, rudely constructed of logs, the windows partly glazed, and partly patched with leaves of old copybooks.

K'BOCKER 4: The low murmur of his pupils' voices, conning over their lessons, might be heard on a drowsy summer day like the hum of a beehive.

K'BOCKER 3: Interrupted now and then by the voice of the master or the appalling sound of the birch rod.

SOUND B: (*A thin narrow branch strikes wood*)

ICHABOD: The golden maxim—"Spare the rod and spoil the child!"

PEDAGOGUE 1: Yet, it behooved him to keep on good terms with his pupils, especially those with mothers noted for the comforts of the cupboard.

PEDAGOGUE 2: You see, the school salary was small.

K'BOCKER 4: And he was a huge feeder, with the dilating powers of an anaconda. He boarded and lodged with the families of farmers, whose children he instructed—living a week at a time with them—going the rounds, with all his worldly effects tied up in a cotton handkerchief.

K'BOCKER 1: He rendered himself useful and agreeable, assisting the farmers occasionally, petting the children, even rocking the cradle for hours.

ICHABOD: In addition, he was singing master of the neighborhood and church.

K'BOCKER 2: And on Sundays, leading the singing of the hymns, his voice resounded far above the rest of the congregation. It is said that his peculiar quavers are still heard in that church.

K'BOCKER 3: And which may be heard half a mile off—quavers descended from the nose of Ichabod Crane.

PEDAGOGUE 1: The schoolmaster is generally a man of some importance in the female circle of a rural neighborhood, being considered gentlemanlike and of vast superior taste and accomplishments—indeed, he is thought to be inferior in learning only to the parson.

PEDAGOGUE 2: He had read several books quite through.

PEDAGOGUE 2: He'd mastered Cotton Mather's *The History of New England Witchcraft*—which he most firmly and potently believed.

ICHABOD: No tale was too gross or monstrous for him to swallow.

K'BOCKER 2: But in the evening, after reading old Mather's direful tales, every sound of nature fluttered his excited imagination.

SOUNDS A-C: (*Sounds of whippoorwill, tree toad, screech owl, rustle of branches*)

K'BOCKER 3: And, if by chance a beetle flew into him by mistake, poor Ichabod knew he'd been struck by a witch's token!

K'BOCKER 1: Yet he took fearful pleasures in hearing stories of the Headless Horseman. Then he would frighten those storytellers with his own speculations upon comets and shooting stars and with the alarming fact that the world did absolutely turn around, and that half the time they were topsy-turvy.

SOUND A: (*Horse plods along*)

K'BOCKER 3: But what fearful shapes and shadows beset his path in the dim and ghastly glare of a snowy night. How often was he appalled by some shrub covered with snow—like a sheeted spectre. How often did he shrink from the sound of his own footsteps—or some rushing blast!

SOUND D: (*Sound of wild wind*)

K'BOCKER 2: Luckily, daylight put an end to these evils.

K'BOCKER 1: Then, one day, his path was crossed by a Being that causes more trouble to mortal man than all the ghosts, goblins, and witches put together—and that Being was a young woman, Katrina Van Tassel.

KATRINA: Daughter and only child of Baltus Van Tassel—a blooming lass, plump as a partridge, and as rosy-cheeked as a peach.

KATRINA: She soon found favor in the eyes of Ichabod—

ICHABOD: Especially after he visited her in her father's mansion.

MR. VAN: Baltus Van Tassel was a perfect picture of a thriving, contented, liberal-hearted farmer. He seldom, it is true, sent his eyes—or his thoughts—beyond his own farm, but within those boundaries, everything was snug, happy, and well-conditioned.

K'BOCKER 2: He was satisfied with his wealth, but not proud of it.

K'BOCKER 1: As the enraptured Ichabod fancied all Mr. Van Tassel owned, his heart yearned after the damsel who was to inherit these domains.

K'BOCKER 2: From that moment on, the peace of his mind was at an end. His only study was how to gain the affections of the peerless daughter of Van Tassel. In this enterprise, he faced real difficulties.

PEDAGOGUE 1: He had to win the heart of this country coquette—Katrina.

PEDAGOGUE 2: He had to encounter fearful adversaries of real flesh and blood—her many village admirers ready to fly out against any new competitor.

K'BOCKER 3: Among these was a burly, roaring, roistering blade by the name of Abraham—or according to the Dutch abbreviation, Brom Van Brunt.

ICHABOD: He was the hero of the country, broad-shouldered, and double-jointed.

KATRINA: And he had short, curly black hair.

ICHABOD: Big and powerful as Hercules, he was known as Brom Bones.

KATRINA: He had great knowledge and skill in horsemanship, too, and was foremost at all the races.

MR. VAN: He was always ready for either a fight or a frolic. He had more mischief than ill will, though. Rough, you see, but with good humor.

KATRINA: We looked upon him with awe and admiration.

K'BOCKER 3: When any madcap prank or rustic brawl occurred in the vicinity, the neighbors shook their heads.

MR. VAN: I warrant Bram Bones was at the bottom of that!

K'BOCKER1: This wild, boisterous fellow, this rantipole hero—had for some time, singled out Katrina Van Tassel as the object of his gallantries.

KATRINA: She did not, altogether, discourage his hopes.

HISTORIAN 2: Such was the formidable rival with whom Ichabod had to contend.

ICHABOD: To take the field openly against Brom Bones would be madness. After all, this lion was not a man to be thwarted in his amours.

MRS. VAN: Ichabod made his advances in a quiet manner. In his character of the singing master, he made frequent visits to the farmhouse.

K'BOCKER 1: Not that he had to fear interference from Katrina's parents.

MR. VAN: Balt Van Tassel loved his daughter better than his pipe. So, like a reasonable man and an excellent father, he let Katrina have her way in everything.

K'BOCKER 2: His notable little wife, too. She had enough to do—attend to her housekeeping and manage her poultry.

MRS. VAN: Ducks and geese are foolish things, and must be looked after, but girls can take care of themselves.

K'BOCKER 1: Thus, while the busy dame bustled about the house, honest Balt would sit smoking his pipe and watching the weathervane on his barn fight with the wind.

K'BOCKER 1: In the meantime, Ichabod would carry on his suit with the daughter—by the side of the spring, under the giant elm, or sauntering along in the twilight.

K'BOCKER 3: Now, from the moment Ichabod Crane made his advances to Katrina, a deadly feud began to grow between Brom Bones and the principal of the Sleepy Hollow school.

K'BOCKER 4: Ichabod was conscious of the superior strength of his adversary.

ICHABOD: Besides, he had overheard Bones boast that he would "double the schoolmaster up and lay him on a shelf of his own schoolhouse."

MRS. VAN: Bones and his gang of rough riders began to play boorish, practical jokes. Once, they smoked out his school by stopping up the chimney.

MR. VAN: Broke into the schoolhouse one night, turning everything topsy-turvy.

KATRINA: Ichabod began to think all the witches in the country held their meetings there, in the schoolhouse.

K'BOCKER 1: Matters went on for some time, without any real effect on the situation—until an invitation was delivered to the schoolhouse door.

ICHABOD: An invitation to a merrymaking—a quilting frolic to be held that evening at Mynheer Van Tassel's!

PEDAGOGUE: All was now bustle and hubbub in the schoolroom. The scholars were hurried through their lessons, and the whole school was turned loose an hour before the usual time.

K'BOCKER 2: The gallant Ichabod spent at least an extra half hour, brushing and furbishing his best—and only—suit of rusty black. Then he arranged his looks in the bit of looking glass that hung in the schoolroom.

PEDAGOGUE 1: Next, to appear before Katrina in the true style of a cavalier, he borrowed a horse from the farmer where he was living.

MR. VAN: This animal was a broken-down plow horse—gaunt and shagged—with a head like a hammer.

GUNPOWDER: His rusty mane and tail were tangled and knotted with burrs. One eye had lost its pupil, but the other had the gleam of a genuine devil in it.

ICHABOD: He bore the name of Gunpowder and had the lurking devil in him.

From *Readers Theatre for Middle School Boys: Investigating the Strange and Mysterious* by Ann N. Black. Westport, CT: Teacher Ideas Press. Copyright © 2008.

K'BOCKER 1: Certainly Ichabod was a suitable figure for such a steed.

GUNPOWDER: He rode with short stirrups, which brought his knees nearly up to the pommel of the saddle. His sharp elbows stuck out like grasshoppers, and his arms went flapping like a pair of wings.

K'BOCKER 2: A small wool hat rested on top of his nose (as the scanty strip of his forehead might be called), and the skirts of his black coat fluttered almost to the horse's tail. Such was the appearance of Ichabod and his steed as they shambled out.

K'BOCKER 1: It was an apparition as is seldom to be met in broad daylight.

K'BOCKER 3: But it was a fine autumnal day as Ichabod jogged slowly on his way.

ICHABOD: On all sides—vast stores of apples, fields of Indian corn, yellow pumpkins, and buckwheat. He breathed the odor of the beehive and thought of flapjacks, buttered and garnished with honey, by Katrina.

K'BOCKER 4: It was toward evening that Ichabod arrived at Heer Van Tassel's home, already thronged with all the pride and flower of the country.

K'BOCKER 3: Brom Bones, however, was the hero of the scene, having come to the gathering on his favorite steed Daredevil—like him, full of mischief.

K'BOCKER 2: Entering the parlor, a world of charms burst upon the enraptured gaze of Ichabod. Not the bevy of buxom lasses, but the ample charms of the Dutch country tea table, heaped with platters of cakes and pies.

ICHABOD: He could not help rolling his large eyes around him as he ate and chuckling with the possibility that he might one day be lord of all this scene of unimaginable luxury and splendor.

MR. VAN: Old Baltus Van Tassel moved among his guests with a face dilated with content and good humor, round and jolly as the harvest moon.

KATRINA 1: Before long, the sound of music summoned the guests to the dance.

ICHABOD: Ichabod prided himself upon his dancing as much as he did upon his vocal powers. Not a limb, not a fiber about him was idle as he danced.

K'BOCKER 2: To have seen his loosely hung frame in full motion, clattering about the room, you would have thought Saint Vitus himself, that blessed patron of the dance, was before you in person.

K'BOCKER 1: Katrina, the lady of his heart, was his partner in the dance—while Brom Bones, smitten with jealousy, sat brooding in one corner.

HISTORIAN 1: When the dance was at an end, Ichabod was drawn to a knot of old folks who were gossiping over former times and telling stories—tales of the supernatural—of ghosts and funeral trains and apparitions.

HISTORIAN 2: The chief part of the stories, however, turned upon the favorite specter of Sleepy Hollow—the headless horseman who had been heard several times of late, patrolling the country, and, it was said, who tethered his horse every night among the graves in the churchyard.

HISTORIAN 1: There was the tale of one man who had followed this headless horseman over hill and swamp—until the specter suddenly turned into a skeleton and sprang over the treetops with a clap of thunder.

K'BOCKER 3: Then Brom Bones told how he had met the horseman one night—and had offered to race him—but just as they came to the church bridge, the Hessian bolted and vanished in a flash of fire.

From *Readers Theatre for Middle School Boys: Investigating the Strange and Mysterious* by Ann N. Black. Westport, CT: Teacher Ideas Press. Copyright © 2008.

K'BOCKER 1: Well, the revel gradually broke up, and before long, the late scene of noise and frolic was silent and deserted.

ICHABOD: But Ichabod, convinced of his success with the heiress, Katrina, lingered behind to have a tête-à-tête with her.

HISTORIAN 2: Something, however, must have gone wrong.

K'BOCKER 1: In a short time he came out quite desolate, chapfallen—depressed.

K'BOCKER 2: He went straight to the stable, and with several kicks roused his steed.

SOUND A: (*Horse whinnies in objection. Horse then begins to plod slowly.*)

K'BOCKER 4: (*Scary*) It was the very witching time of night—dismal and dead.

K'BOCKER 2: As Ichabod rode along, he could hear sounds from far off.

SOUNDS: (*In succession: A brief pause between each sound as previous one fades away: barking dog, cock crows, cricket chirps, bullfrog belch.*)

ICHABOD: The night grew darker and darker. The stars seemed to sink deeper in the sky, and driving clouds occasionally hid them from sight. (*Scared*)

He was approaching the giant tulip tree.

PEDAGOGUE 2: The tree where they had hanged Major André, the Revolutionary spy.

ICHABOD: He began to whistle. He was coming to the stream.

SOUNDS: (*Weak whistling fades into the sound of a rush of wind*)

PEDAGOGUE 2: It was the haunted stream, where they had captured Major André.

ICHABOD: (*Fearfully*) He had to pass over that bridge that crossed that stream. His heart began to thump. He kicked and kicked his horse in the ribs.

GUNPOWDER: But instead of dashing across the bridge, Gunpowder plunged into a thicket of brambles. The schoolmaster bestowed both whip and heel upon old Gunpowder.

SOUND A: (*Plodding horse begins to run, then, on line below, stops abruptly*)

GUNPOWDER: Gunpowder then dashed forward, snuffling and snorting—only to stop suddenly, nearly sending his rider sprawling over his head.

K'BOCKER 2: Just at that moment, Ichabod heard something—and he beheld something—huge, misshapen, black, and towering—some gigantic monster ready to spring.

K'BOCKER 1: The hair of the frightened pedagogue rose upon his head in terror.

ICHABOD: What was to be done? To turn and fly was now too late. Besides, what chance was there of escaping a ghost or goblin which could ride upon the wings of the wind? (*Pause*) "Who are you? Who are you?"

K'BOCKER 1: The shadow of alarm put itself in motion. With a scramble and a bound, it stood at once in the middle of the road.

K'BOCKER 4: He appeared to be a horseman of large dimensions.

ICHABOD: And mounted on a black horse of powerful frame.

K'BOCKER 2: Ichabod had no relish for this strange midnight companion, and he reminded himself of the adventure Brom Bones had with the specter.

K'BOCKER 1: Hoping to leave the creatures behind, Ichabod quickened his steed.

SOUND A: (*Horse hooves running fast*)

K'BOCKER 3: The stranger quickened his horse to an equal pace.

SOUND B: (*Another horse running fast*)

K'BOCKER 1: Ichabod fell into a walk.

K'BOCKER 3: The horseman did the same.

SOUNDS A, B: (*Horses slow to a walk*)

ICHABOD: His heart began to sink. He endeavored to resume singing one of the hymns, but he could not utter a note. (*Pause*) Then he saw it!

K'BOCKER 4: Saw his fellow-traveler outlined in relief against the sky. It was gigantic in height and muffled in a cloak. Ichabod was horror-struck!

ICHABOD: The stranger was headless! And the head, which should have rested on his shoulders, was carried before him on the pommel of his saddle.

K'BOCKER 1: Ichabod's terror rose to desperation.

ICHABOD: He rained a shower of kicks and blows upon Gunpowder, hoping to give his companion the slip—but the specter jumped with him!

K' BOCKER 2: Away then they dashed, stones flying! Sparks flashing in the air.

SOUND: (*Horses galloping. Sounds slowly fade.*)

ICHABOD: Ichabod's flimsy garments fluttered in the air as he stretched his long, lank body over his horse's head, in the eagerness of his flight.

GUNPOWDER: Gunpowder seemed possessed with a demon—but instead of turning onto the Sleepy Hollow road, he made an opposite turn and plunged headlong downhill to the left.

HISTORIAN 1: This road crosses a bridge, then leads up to the grassy knoll on which stands the whitewashed church.

K'BOCKER 2: So far, the panic of the steed had given his unskilled rider, Ichabod, an apparent advantage in the

From *Readers Theatre for Middle School Boys: Investigating the Strange and Mysterious* by Ann N. Black. Westport, CT: Teacher Ideas Press. Copyright © 2008.

chase—but just as he was halfway there, the girths holding the saddle gave way.

ICHABOD: He felt the saddle slipping! He seized it by the pommel and endeavored to hold it firm, but in vain. To save himself, he clasped old Gunpowder around the neck—and the saddle fell to the earth.

K' BOCKER 1: He heard it being trampled on by his pursuer. The goblin was hard on his haunches. He had to try to maintain his seat on Gunpowder!

K' BOCKER 2: But Ichabod was slipping on one side—then the other, jolting on the horse's backbone with such violence that he was almost sliced in two.

K'BOCKER 3: Then an opening in the trees cheered him. He saw the bridge to the church ahead and the whitewashed walls of the church. He recollected now—the church bridge was where Brom Bones's ghostly competitor had disappeared.

ICHABOD: If I can but reach that bridge—I am safe.

K'BOCKER 4: Just then, he heard the black steed panting and blowing close behind him, and he fancied he felt its hot breath.

K'BOCKER 2: He gave old Gunpowder another kick in the ribs, and he sprang upon the bridge, thundered across, and gained the opposite side.

K'BOCKER 1: Ichabod cast a look behind to see if his pursuer would vanish—according to rule—in a flash of fire and brimstone.

ICHABOD: But just then, he saw the goblin rising in his stirrups—and in the very act of hurling his head at him!

K'BOCKER 1: Ichabod endeavored to dodge the horrible missile—but too late!

ICHABOD: The thing hit his cranium with a tremendous crash—and he tumbled headlong into the dust.

From *Readers Theatre for Middle School Boys: Investigating the Strange and Mysterious* by Ann N. Black. Westport, CT: Teacher Ideas Press. Copyright © 2008.

K'BOCKER 3: (*Slowly*) Gunpowder—and the black steed—and the goblin-rider all passed him by like a whirlwind.

HISTORIAN 1: (*Pause*) The next morning the old horse was found—but Ichabod did not make his appearance at breakfast—or at dinner. No Ichabod.

PEDAGOGUE 2: The boys assembled at the schoolhouse, but no schoolmaster.

HISTORIAN 2: An inquiry was set, and after diligent investigation, they came upon his traces. Then they found the saddle, trampled in the dirt.

HISTORIAN 1: They followed the tracks of the horses' hooves to the bridge, and where the brook ran deep and black—there, they found his hat.

HISTORIAN 2: And close beside the hat, they found—a shattered pumpkin!

K'BOCKER 1: The brook was searched, but the body of the schoolmaster was not to be discovered. After much speculation, they came to the conclusion that Ichabod had been carried off by the galloping Hessian.

K'BOCKER 3: Brom Bones, however, was observed to look knowingly whenever the story of Ichabod was related, and he always burst into a hearty laugh at the mention of that pumpkin.

HISTORIAN 1: This, of course, led some people to suspect that Brom knew more about the matter than he chose to tell.

HISTORIAN 2: Some years later, it was said that the schoolmaster was alive in a distant part of the country, had studied law and turned politician.

K'BOCKER 1: The old country wives, however, who are the best judges of these matters, maintain to this day that Ichabod was spirited away by supernatural means.

PEDAGOGUE 1: Well, I must confess—the story seems a little extravagant to me. There are one or two points on which I have my doubts.

K' BOCKER 1: Faith, sir, as to that matter, I don't believe half of it myself.

K' BOCKER 2: Nor I!

K' BOCKER 3: Nor I!

K'BOCKER 4: Nor I!

STUDENT: Nor I! But I must confess, too. Sleepy Hollow's a great story, after all—thanks to Washington Irving.

K'BOCKERS 1–4: (*All bow to Student and speak together*) Thank you!

Beware! "The Monkey's Paw" by W. W. Jacobs

Just mention that famous short story "The Monkey's Paw" and you're sure to engender a great response. Eyes widen and people shudder, for this is a tale to terrify and to remind us: be careful what you wish for. Cast in the mode of a folktale by the Brothers Grimm, "The Monkey's Paw," though more than one hundred years old, remains popular today. Indeed, the story has been dramatized and filmed frequently, both here and abroad.

The author, William Wymark Jacobs, came from humble beginnings. Born in the environs of London, England, in 1863, Jacobs spent much of his early life around the docks of Wapping where his father managed one of the wharves. Marine life became *his* life, providing a rich background for his subjects and inspiring many of his stories.

Having grown up in straitened circumstances and having left school at sixteen, Jacobs gravitated to a steady, dependable position as a clerk. But that was not enough for him. He began to write and to submit his humorous stories to magazines. Soon acclaimed for his droll humor, critics often compared his work to that of Charles Dickens.

All his stories have an edge, a twist, and, frequently, satire. Later, as in "The Monkey's Paw," Jacobs added elements of horror and suspense to his stories. Still later, as a popular playwright, he joined the prestigious Dramatists Club in London alongside such luminaries as J. M. Barrie, George Bernard Shaw, and P. G. Wodehouse.

Although politically conservative, Jacobs married a suffragette, Agnes Eleanor Williams, and together they raised four children. Jacobs enjoyed a long life and a successful career, dying at the age of eighty in 1943, within that large circle of London.

Even as we reject the magic of a mysterious, gruesome talisman, we turn with scared delight to read "The Monkey's Paw"—just one more time.

PRODUCTION NOTES

Oh, we all know "it's just a story!" It couldn't be true, could it? There's no such thing as a magic monkey's paw—much less the tantalizing prospect of three wishes.

All thoughts true—except that W. W. Jacobs recognized the frailty of human nature and, with great imagination, wrote about it—immortalized it in his short stories, perhaps the most famous being "The Monkey's Paw."

This Readers Theatre script provides an innovative way to introduce the elements of fear and greed and fate that influence the characters and the plot of Jacobs's short story. At the outset, we meet ordinary people with ordinary names—Mr. and Mrs. White and their son, Herbert. The first visitor is Morris. The second, and the bearer of tragic news, has no name. Only the firm he represents has a name—Maw and Meggins, as impersonal as a box of soap.

Eleven readers make up the cast, only one of which, the Wife, should be played by a female. Definitely male roles include the Husband, Herbert, the Major, and the Visitor. The parts of the six Narrators can be read by either boys or girls.

Sound effects can add a great deal of tension to the presentation of "The Monkey's Paw." Four crew members, Sounds A, B, C, and D, share these responsibilities.

In general, the sounds can be improvised and produced orally. However, suggestions for other methods can be found in the Sound Appendix. It is, of course, possible to present the script without sound effects.

Altogether, the cast and crew will be made up of fifteen participants.

The production requires fifteen scripts, plus one for the teacher.

Beware! "The Monkey's Paw" by W. W. Jacobs

```
Sounds A, B                              Sounds C, D
   X X                                      X X

          Major                     Visitor
            X                          X
Narrators                                    Narrators
   X3                                           X6
   X2             Herbert                       X5
             Wife       X       Husband         X4
   X1          X               X
```

NARRATOR 1: (*Mysterious tones*) It was a dark and stormy night!

NARRATOR 6: Oh, please! We've all heard that one!

NARRATOR 1: Outside a little home in a small English village, the wind blew furiously. "Without," Jacobs writes, "the night was cold and wet."

From *Readers Theatre for Middle School Boys: Investigating the Strange and Mysterious* by Ann N. Black. Westport, CT: Teacher Ideas Press. Copyright © 2008.

NARRATOR 6: Oh, sorry! You're really serious. What's the story? Is it spooky?

NARRATOR 4: (*Laughs*) Oh, I think you could say that. It's a little chilling.

NARRATOR 1: And ominous! The story's "The Monkey's Paw"—by William Wymark Jacobs—born in England during the reign of Queen Victoria—

NARRATOR 4: Who was also the Queen of India. Maybe that's why the English were so fascinated by that country—it was so far away, so different. India seemed to be all things mysterious and magical.

NARRATOR 1: Correct! Soldiers and adventurers came back to England with wonderful stories to tell.

NARRATOR 5: I understand where this is going, but can we get on with the story?

NARRATOR 3: Let me start.

SOUNDS A, B: (*Winds begin to blow*)

NARRATOR 2: Let me set the scene: Mr. and Mrs. White and their son, Herbert, are sitting before the fire in their little cottage. Mrs. White is knitting. Father and son are playing chess. They are waiting for a visitor.

HUSBAND: Hark at the wind!

HERBERT: I'm listening, father.

HUSBAND: I should hardly think he'd come tonight. That's the worst of living so far out. The path is a bog, and the road's a torrent. I suppose because only two houses in the road are rented, they think it doesn't matter!

WIFE: Never mind, dear, don't be upset. Perhaps you'll win the next game.

NARRATOR 2: Mr. White looked up sharply, just in time to intercept a knowing glance between mother and son.

	Chess game, indeed! Still, his heated words died away, and he hid a guilty grin in his thin gray beard.
SOUNDS A, B:	(*Winds begin to die down*)
SOUNDS C, D:	(*Heavy footsteps, then a knock on the door*)
HERBERT:	Well, there he is!
SOUND C:	(*Door opens and closes*)
SOUNDS A, B:	(*Winds stop*)
HUSBAND:	Meet my friend, Sergeant-Major Morris! Twenty-one years gone. When he went away he was a slip of a youth in the warehouse. Now look at him. I'd like to go to India myself—just to look around a bit.
MAJOR:	Better where you are.
HUSBAND:	I should like to see those old temples and fakirs and jugglers. What was that you started telling me the other day about a monkey's paw or something, Morris?
MAJOR:	Nothing. Nothing—leastways nothing worth hearing.
WIFE:	(*Curiously*) Did you say a monkey's paw?
MAJOR:	Well, it's just a bit of what you might call magic, perhaps. To look at, it's just an ordinary little paw, dried to a mummy.
NARRATOR 3:	He took something from his pocket and held it out before him. Mrs. White drew back with a grimace, but her son took it and examined it curiously.
HUSBAND:	And what is there special about it?
MAJOR:	It had a spell put on it by an old fakir—a very holy man. He wanted to show that fate ruled people's lives, and that those who interfered with fate did so to their sorrow. He put a spell on it so that three separate men could each have three wishes. I am the second man to own it.

From *Readers Theatre for Middle School Boys: Investigating the Strange and Mysterious* by Ann N. Black. Westport, CT: Teacher Ideas Press. Copyright © 2008.

HERBERT: (*Slight laugh*) Well, if you own it now, don't you have three wishes?

MAJOR: Ah, you see, I have had.

WIFE: Did you really have the three wishes granted?

MAJOR: Yes—yes, I did.

WIFE: And has anybody else wished?

MAJOR: The first man had his three wishes. I don't know what the first two were, but the third was for death. That's how I got the paw.

HUSBAND: If you've had your three wishes, it's no good to you now, Morris. What do you keep it for?

MAJOR: Fancy, I suppose. I did have some idea of selling it, but I don't think I will. It's caused enough mischief already. Besides, people won't buy. They think it's a fairy tale—some of them. And those who do think anything of it—they want to try it first and pay me afterward.

HUSBAND: If you could have another three wishes—would you have them?

MAJOR: I don't know. (*Pause*) I don't know.

NARRATOR 2: He took the paw, and dangling it between his forefinger and thumb, suddenly threw it upon the fire. Mr. White cried out, stooped down, and snatched it off.

MAJOR: Better let it burn!

HUSBAND: If you don't want it, Morris, give it to me.

MAJOR: I won't. If you keep it, don't blame me for what happens. Pitch it on the fire again like a sensible man.

HUSBAND: (*Shakes his head*) No. No. Now, how do you do it—make the wishes?

MAJOR: Hold it up in your right hand and wish aloud—but I warn you of the consequences. If you must wish, wish for something sensible.

NARRATOR 5: Mr. White dropped the talisman into his pocket. In the business of eating supper, the talisman was partly forgotten, and afterward, the three sat enthralled, listening to the soldier's adventures in India.

SOUND C: (*Door opens, then closes*)

NARRATOR 4: But when the door closed behind their guest, just in time to catch the last train back to London, Herbert smiled at his parents.

HERBERT: If the tale about the monkey's paw is not more truthful than those tales he has been telling us, we shan't make much from it.

WIFE: Did you give him anything for it, father?

HUSBAND: Oh—just a trifle. He didn't want it, but I made him take it. And he pressed me again to throw it away.

HERBERT: Why, we're going to be rich, and famous, and happy! Wish to be an emperor, father, to begin with.

HUSBAND: I don't know what to wish for, and that's a fact. It seems to me I've got all I want.

HERBERT: If you only cleared the house from debt, you'd be quite happy, wouldn't you? Well, wish for two hundred pounds, then. That'll do it.

NARRATOR 1: His father, smiling at his own readiness to believe, held up the talisman. His son, with a solemn face—somewhat marred by a wink to his mother—sat down at the piano and struck a few impressive chords.

HUSBAND: I wish—for two hundred pounds.

NARRATOR 1: A fine crash of music greeted those words—then a shuddering cry from the old man. His wife and son

From *Readers Theatre for Middle School Boys: Investigating the Strange and Mysterious* by Ann N. Black. Westport, CT: Teacher Ideas Press. Copyright © 2008.

ran toward him. The old man looked with disgust at the dried up object that lay on the floor.

HUSBAND: It moved! As I made my wish, it twisted in my hand like a snake!

HERBERT: Well, I don't see the money, and I bet I never shall.

WIFE: It must have been your fancy, Father.

HUSBAND: (*Shakes his head*) No. Never mind, though. No harm done. (*Pause*) But it gave me a shock all the same.

NARRATOR 3: They sat down by the fire again while the father and his son finished smoking their pipes. Outside, the wind was higher than ever.

SOUNDS A, B, C: (*Wind blows. Door begins to bang.*)

NARRATOR 2: The old man started nervously at the sound of a door banging upstairs.

NARRATOR 1: A silence—unusual and depressing—settled upon all three, which lasted until the old couple rose to retire for the night.

HERBERT: Good night. I expect you'll find the cash tied up in a bag in the middle of your bed—and something horrible watching as you pocket your ill-gotten gains.

NARRATOR 5: But once they were gone, Herbert sat alone in the darkness, gazing at the fire, seeing faces in it.

NARRATOR 4: The last face was so horrible—so simian—that he gazed at it with amazement. The face became so vivid that he felt on the table for a glass with a little water to throw over it.

NARRATOR 5: His hand grasped the monkey's paw.

NARRATOR 4: He shivered, wiped his hand on his coat, and went up to bed.

SOUND D: (*Dishes and silverware rattle softly*)

NARRATOR 1: The next morning at breakfast—in the brightness of the wintery sun—Herbert laughed at his fears and at the dirty, shriveled little paw pitched carelessly on the sideboard.

WIFE: I suppose all old soldiers are the same. The idea of our listening to such nonsense! How could wishes be granted in these days? And if they could, how could two hundred pounds hurt you, Father?

HERBERT: (*Light laugh*) Well—it might drop from the sky onto Father's head.

HUSBAND: Ah. Morris said the things happen so naturally that you might, if you so wished, attribute their happening to coincidence.

HERBERT: Well, don't break into the money until I come back. (*Laughs*) I'm afraid it will turn you into a mean, avaricious man, and then we'll have to disown you.

NARRATOR 3: His mother laughed, and following him to the door, watched as he strode down the road. Then, at day's end, the old couple sat, eating their dinner.

WIFE: Herbert will have some more of his funny remarks, I expect, when he comes home for dinner.

HUSBAND: I dare say.

SOUND D: (*Sound of liquid being poured into a glass*)

NARRATOR 6: Mr. White poured himself out some more beer.

HUSBAND: But for all of that, the Thing moved in my hand. That I will swear to.

WIFE: (*Soothingly*) Well, you thought it did.

HUSBAND: I say it did! There was no thought about it. I had just—(*Stops*) why, what's the matter?

NARRATOR 4: His wife made no reply. She was watching the mysterious movements of a man outside, peering at their house. He appeared to be trying to make up his mind to enter.

From *Readers Theatre for Middle School Boys: Investigating the Strange and Mysterious* by Ann N. Black. Westport, CT: Teacher Ideas Press. Copyright © 2008.

NARRATOR 5: Now, in mental connection with their talk of the two hundred pounds, she noticed that the stranger was well-dressed, and he wore a top hat of glossy newness.

NARRATOR 4: Three times he paused at the gate—then walked on again.

NARRATOR 5: On the fourth time, with a sudden resolution, he flung the gate open and walked up the path.

NARRATOR 6: Mrs. White, at the same moment, hurriedly unfastened the strings on her apron and put that useful article beneath the cushion of her chair.

SOUNDS C: (*Knock on door. Door opens and closes.*)

NARRATOR 6: Mrs. White brought the stranger into the room.

NARRATOR 3: He seemed ill at ease—had a furtive look when he gazed at her—and listened to her in a preoccupied fashion.

NARRATOR 2: She apologized for the appearance of the room—and for the appearance of her husband's coat—a garment he usually reserved for the garden.

NARRATOR 3: She then waited—as patiently as she could—but the stranger was, at first, strangely silent.

NARRATOR 2: He stooped and picked something—a piece of cotton—from his trousers.

VISITOR: (*Clears his throat*) I come from Maw and Meggins.

WIFE: Oh! (*Pause*) Is anything the matter? Has anything happened to Herbert? What is it? What is it?

HUSBAND: There, there, Mother. Sit down, and don't jump to conclusions. You've not brought bad news, I'm sure, sir.

VISITOR: (*Slight cough*) I'm—I'm sorry. . . .

WIFE: Oh! Oh, is he hurt?

VISITOR: (*Bows head briefly*) Badly hurt—but he's not in any pain.

WIFE: Oh, thank God! Thank God for that! Thank. . . .

NARRATOR 1: Suddenly the sinister meaning dawned upon her. She saw the awful confirmation of her fears in the man's averted face. She caught her breath, turned to her husband, laid her trembling old hand upon his.

NARRATOR 4: There was a long silence. Finally—

VISITOR: (*Quietly*) He was caught in the machinery.

HUSBAND: (*Stunned*) Caught—in the machinery. Yes.

NARRATOR 4: (*Slowly*) The old man sat—staring blankly out the window. Then taking his wife's hand, he pressed it, as he had been wont to do in their courting days, nearly forty years before.

HUSBAND: He was the only one left to us. It is hard.

NARRATOR 1: The visitor coughed—rose—walked slowly to the window—did not look around.

VISITOR: The firm wished me to convey their sincere sympathy with you in your great loss. I beg that you will understand I am only their servant and merely obeying orders.

NARRATOR 3: There was no reply. The old woman's face was white, her eyes staring. Her breath seemed to have stopped.

NARRATOR 6: On the husband's face was a look such as his friend, the sergeant, might have worn—into his first battle.

VISITOR: I was to say that Maw and Meggins disclaim all responsibility. They admit no liability at all. But, in consideration of your son's services, they wish to present you with a certain sum as compensation.

SOUND B: (*A bag of coins drops on the table*)

From *Readers Theatre for Middle School Boys: Investigating the Strange and Mysterious* by Ann N. Black. Westport, CT: Teacher Ideas Press. Copyright © 2008.

NARRATOR 5: Mr. White dropped his wife's hand. Rising to his feet, he gazed with horror at his visitor. His dry lips shaped the words.

HUSBAND: How much? How much?

VISITOR: (*Clears his throat*) Two hundred pounds.

SOUND B: (*Coins spill slowly to the floor*)

NARRATOR 1: Unconscious of his wife's shriek, the old man smiled faintly—put out his hands like a sightless man—and dropped, senseless to the floor.

NARRATOR 4: (*Brief pause*) In the huge new cemetery, some two miles distant, the two old people buried their dead son, then came back to their house, steeped in shadow and silence.

NARRATOR 5: It was all over so quickly that at first they could hardly realize it.

NARRATOR 4: They remained in a state of expectation—as though of something else to happen—something else which would lighten this load, too heavy for old hearts to bear.

NARRATOR 6: But the days passed and expectation gave place to resignation. They hardly exchanged a word. They had nothing to talk about.

NARRATOR 3: About a week after, the old man, waking suddenly in the night, stretched out his hand and found himself alone. The room was in darkness, and the sound of subdued weeping came from the window.

HUSBAND: (*Quietly, kindly*) Come back. You will be cold.

WIFE: (*Short sobs*) It is colder for my son.

NARRATOR 2: The sound of her sobs died away on his ears. His eyes were heavy with sleep. The bed was warm. He dozed fitfully until a sudden wild cry from his wife awoke him with a start.

WIFE: The paw! The monkey's paw!

HUSBAND: Where? Where is it? What's the matter?

WIFE: I want it. You've not destroyed it?

HUSBAND: No. It's in the parlour, on the bracket. Why?

WIFE: (*Strange laughter*) I only just thought of it. Why didn't I think of it before? Why didn't *you* think of it?

HUSBAND: Of what? Think of what?

WIFE: The other two wishes! We've only had one.

HUSBAND: Wasn't that enough?!!

WIFE: No. No! We'll have one more. Go down and get it quickly—and wish our boy alive again!

HUSBAND: Good God, you are mad!

WIFE: Get it! Get it quickly and wish—oh, my boy! My boy!

NARRATOR 1: The man sat up in bed and flung the bedclothes from his quaking limbs. He struck a match and lit the candle.

HUSBAND: Get back to bed. You don't know what you're saying!

WIFE: We had the first wish granted—why not the second?

HUSBAND: A coincidence. A coincidence!

WIFE: Go and get it—and wish!

HUSBAND: Mother—he has been dead ten days, and besides he—I would not tell you more, but—I could only recognize him by his clothing. If he was too terrible for you to see him then, how now?

WIFE: Bring him back! Do you think I fear my own child?

NARRATOR 1: The old man went down in the darkness and felt his way to the parlour, then to the mantelpiece. The talisman was in its place.

NARRATOR 3: A horrible fear seized him—that the unspoken wish might bring his mutilated son before him—ere he could escape from the room.

NARRATOR 2: He caught his breath. He'd lost direction of the door! His brow, cold with sweat, he felt his way around the table until he found himself in the small hallway with the unwholesome thing in his hand.

NARRATOR 4: As he entered the room, even his wife's face seemed changed. It was white and expectant. (*Pause*) He was afraid of her.

WIFE: Wish!

HUSBAND: It is foolish and wicked.

WIFE: Wish!

NARRATOR 5: He raised his hand.

HUSBAND: I—I wish my son alive again.

NARRATOR 6: The talisman fell to the floor. The man regarded it fearfully, then sank trembling into a chair. The old woman, with burning eyes, walked to the window.

NARRATOR 4: He sat until he was chilled with the cold, glancing occasionally at the old woman peering through the window. The candle-end threw pulsating shadows on the ceiling and the walls until—it expired.

SOUND A: (*Clock begins ticking*)

NARRATOR 1: The old man, relieved at the failure of the talisman, crept back to bed.

NARRATOR 2: A minute or two afterward, the old woman also returned to bed.

NARRATOR 3: They lay silently, listening to the ticking of the clock. A stair creaked. A squeaky mouse scurried noisily through the wall.

SOUND D: (*Squeaky noises*)

From *Readers Theatre for Middle School Boys: Investigating the Strange and Mysterious* by Ann N. Black. Westport, CT: Teacher Ideas Press. Copyright © 2008.

NARRATOR 4: But the darkness was oppressive. Finally the old man took the box of matches and struck one.

SOUND B: (*Match is struck*)

NARRATOR 5: He went downstairs for a candle. At the foot of the stairs, the match went out. He paused to strike another.

SOUND C: (*Three quiet knocks on wood*)

NARRATOR 6: The matches fell from his hand and spilled in the hallway. He stood motionless, his breath suspended—until the knock was repeated.

SOUND C: (*Three more quiet knocks on wood*)

NARRATOR 5: The old man fled swiftly to his room and closed the door behind him.

SOUND C: (*Three louder knocks on wood*)

WIFE: (*Frightened*) Father! What was that?

HUSBAND: A rat—only a rat. It passed me on the stairs.

SOUND C: (*Three loud, slow knocks*)

WIFE: (*Happy and excited*) It's Herbert! It's Herbert!

NARRATOR 1: She ran to the door, but her husband caught her by the arm and held her tightly.

HUSBAND: (*Frantic*) What are you going to do?

WIFE: It's my boy! It's Herbert! I forgot it was two miles away. What are you holding me for? Let go. I must open the door.

HUSBAND: For God's sake don't let it in!

WIFE: You're afraid of your own son. Let me go! (*Calls*) I'm coming, Herbert. I'm coming!

SOUND C: (*Three knocks. Pause. Three more knocks.*)

NARRATOR 2: The old woman suddenly broke free and ran from the room. Her husband followed her to the landing and called after her.

SOUND D, A: (*Chain rattles. Bolt struggles to slide open.*)

WIFE: Oh—the bolt! Come down. I can't reach the bolt.

NARRATOR 3: But her husband was on his hands and knees groping wildly on the floor in search of the paw. If he could only find it—before the thing outside got in!

NARRATOR 1: And then. . .

SOUND C: (A *furious succession of knocks, then a constant, slower series*)

SOUND B: (*Chair scrapes on floor, then thuds against door*)

NARRATOR 1: A terrible barrage of knocks reverberated throughout the house, and he heard the scraping of a chair as his wife put it down in the passageway and against the door.

SOUND A: (*The bolt creaks and slowly slides open*)

NARRATOR 1: The bolt! He heard the creaking of the bolt as it came slowly back.

NARRATOR 4: And at the same moment—he found the monkey's paw, and frantically, he breathed his third—and last wish.

SOUND C: (*Knocking stops*)

NARRATOR 4: The knocking ceased suddenly, although the echoes of it were still in the house.

SOUND D: (*Three faint knocks, as echoes*)

SOUND B: (*Chair scrapes back across the floor*)

SOUND C: (*Door creaks opens. Knocking stops*)

SOUND A, B: (*A long, drawn out rush of wind*)

NARRATOR 1: A cold wind rushed up the staircase. A long, loud wail of disappointment and misery from his wife gave the old man courage to run down to her side—then out to the gate beyond.

NARRATOR 4: (*Slowly*) The streetlamp—flickering opposite—shone on a quiet—and deserted road.

Desperation Grows
"To Light a Fire"
by Jack London

Unbridled passion seemed to drive the genius of a young man who was born in California, unwanted and unclaimed. Jack London, who was illegitimate and impoverished, was nevertheless born with a thirst for knowledge and an insatiable ambition—all qualities that would transform him into one of America's great storytellers.

San Francisco, that spectacular city by the bay, was home to Jack London. He was born there, January 12, 1876. He grew up amid its squalor, worked in its canning factories and laundries, and knew its seamy side. Yet, the city had a library for him, ships in the harbor to tantalize his wanderlust, and schools to seek out and join—for a time.

A stepsister, Eliza, cared for him, and his stepfather, John London, did his best to nurture him. But by the time the boy was sixteen and barely educated, he'd left home and taken to the road. He was a hobo, became a sailor, was arrested for vagrancy and thrown in jail. Then, the 1897 Klondike Gold Rush took him north to the Yukon. He became enmeshed in strong causes and powerful ideas, often shocking those around him. But these quests were all grist for the mill. London was training himself to be a writer.

By 1900, the same day that his first novel was published, the handsome and charismatic London married Bessie Maddern. By 1902 they had two daughters. The marriage did not last, however; and in 1905 Charmian Kittredge, London's adventurous and intellectual soul mate, became his second wife.

Plagued by his unconquerable affinity for alcohol, the brilliant Jack London died at age forty on November 22, 1916, leaving us a treasure of his strong ideas and spellbinding stories.

PRODUCTION NOTES

Jack London was intent upon becoming a writer, and he was serious about developing his craft, his art. Every morning of his life he wrote in longhand up to fifteen hundred words a day. He had things to say that he drew from every event, every relationship of his life, and he brought them to us in essays, letters, novels, and stories.

London wrote tales of the sea, of wars, of struggles with people, battles with the weather. Adventure stories, to be sure, but the derring-do is only the top layer of his work. We may find a few outdated spellings in this text, but London inevitably shows us the strengths and weaknesses of both men and animals, as in his most famous short story "To Light a Fire."

Although the story recounts the experiences of one man and one dog, the following script can use a cast of eight readers and two sound-effects people.

There are no actual dialogues in London's story, but we are privy to what the man is thinking —even to what the dog is thinking. We experience these thoughts through the readers Man 1, Man 2, Man 3, and by all means, Dog.

Narrators 1 through 4 describe the external conditions and the shifting changes of the weather and the terrain that affect the man and the dog. The Narrators show us the courage and the weakness of the two. Consequently, we see, we live through the inevitable disaster as it grows.

Sound effects, taking place in a frozen northland, are slight, but they can be very effective and easily handled. Suggestions for them appear in the Sound Appendix. Of course, the script will be mesmerizing, even without sound effects.

Ten scripts, plus one for the teacher, will be required for the cast and sound crew.

Desperation Grows
"To Light a Fire"
by Jack London

	Sounds A					Sounds B	
	X					X	
Narrators 1 & 2		Man 1	Man 2	Man 3	Dog		Narrators 3 & 4
X X		X	X	X	X		X X

NARRATOR 1: Well, I think it's time for a geography lesson, folks.

MAN 1: Oh, yeah? Speak for yourself. I know where we are—and where we're going—to the frozen north.

MAN 2: And we mean north—the Yukon. We're heading for the Arctic Circle.

MAN 3: You mean Canada—and frozen land—well, especially in the winter.

NARRATOR 2: Oh, good. That's when our hero takes off—and in the dead of winter, so to speak—like Jack London did, too—the author of this story.

MAN 2: Yukon Territory means gold to me—the Klondike and the Gold Rush—bags and bags of glittery dust and big chunks of that gold.

SOUND A: (*A jumble of rocks and thumps of small bags of dirt*)

NARRATOR 3: Pretty exciting time—for a while. It was 1897 when the news broke—Gold! So, Jack London, who was twenty-one years old, left his thirty-dollars-a-month job in a laundry and joined thousands of people from all over the world who rushed to the Klondike River Valley for gold.

MAN 1: He left San Francisco for the frozen north—and lived to tell the tale.

NARRATOR 1: And here it is—we have it—the famous story "To Light a Fire."

SOUND A: (*Bag of coins jingles*)

SOUND B: (*Sound of match striking. Brief crackling of fire.*)

NARRATOR 2: Day had broken cold and gray, exceedingly cold and gray, when the man turned aside from the main Yukon trail and climbed the high earth-bank, where a dim and little-traveled road led eastward through the fat spruce timberland.

NARRATOR 3: It was a steep bank, and he paused for breath at the top, excusing the need to stop, excusing the act to himself by looking at his watch.

MAN 1: Nine o'clock. No sun, nor hint of sun—though not a cloud in the sky.

MAN 2: A clear day. Yet there seemed a subtle gloom that made the day dark.

NARRATOR 4: This fact did not worry the man. He was used to the lack of the sun. He flung a look back—along the way he had come.

MAN 3: The Yukon River lay a mile wide and hidden under three feet of ice and as much of snow. As far as his eye could see, unbroken white—save for a dark hair-line that curved and twisted, then disappeared.

MAN 2: This dark hair-line was the trail—the main trail.

NARRATOR 2: But all this—the mysterious, far-reaching hairline trail, the absence of sun from the sky, the tremendous cold, and the strangeness and the weirdness of it all—made no impression on the man.

NARRATOR 1: It was not because he was used to it. (*Shakes head no*) He was a newcomer in the land. A prospector, and this was his first winter.

NARRATOR 3: The trouble was—he was without imagination.

NARRATOR 4: (*Nods*) He was quick and alert in the things of life, but only in the things—not in the significances.

MAN 1: Fifty degrees below zero meant eighty-odd degrees of frost.

MAN 2: Cold and uncomfortable—a bit of frost that hurt and must be guarded against by mittens, earflaps, warm moccasins, and thick socks.

NARRATOR 2: That there should be anything more to it never entered his head.

MAN 3: At fifty below zero, spittle crackles on the snow. He spat, just to see.

SOUND B: (*Sharp cracking sound*)

MAN 2: He spat again and again.

SOUND B: (*Cracking sounds repeat three times*)

MAN 3: The spittle crackled in the air—before it hit the snow. (*Pause*) It was colder than fifty below—how much he didn't know.

From *Readers Theatre for Middle School Boys: Investigating the Strange and Mysterious* by Ann N. Black. Westport, CT: Teacher Ideas Press. Copyright © 2008.

MAN 1: The temperature didn't matter. He'd be in camp by six o'clock, a bit after dark. The boys would have a fire going and a hot supper ready.

MAN 3: And as for lunch—it was under his shirt, wrapped up in a handkerchief, and lying against his naked skin—the only way to keep the biscuits from freezing.

MAN 2: Smiling, he thought of those biscuits, cut open, sopped in bacon grease, and each enclosing a generous slice of fried bacon.

NARRATOR 1: He plunged in among the spruce trees, but the trail was faint. A foot of snow had fallen since the last sled. He was glad he was without a sled—traveling light, carrying nothing but his lunch.

MAN 3: But it certainly was cold.

MAN 1: He rubbed his numb nose and cheek-bones with his mittened hand.

NARRATOR 3: He was a warm-whiskered man, but the hair on his face did not protect him against the frosty air.

SOUND B: (*Dog panting*)

NARRATOR 2: At the man's heels trotted a dog, a big native husky, the proper wolf-dog, gray-coated, and not unlike its brother, the wild wolf.

NARRATOR 3: The animal was depressed by the tremendous cold.

DOG: It was no time for traveling.

NARRATOR 1: In reality, it was not merely colder than fifty or sixty or seventy below—it was seventy-five below zero.

DOG: The dog didn't know anything about thermometers, but it had instinct that made it slink along and question movements of the man. It wanted fire, or else to burrow under the snow away from the air.

NARRATOR 3: The frozen moisture of its breathing had settled on its fur in a fine powder of frost. Its jowls, muzzle, and eyelashes whitened as well.

NARRATOR 4: The man's red beard and mustache were likewise frosted.

NARRATOR 2: Also, the man was chewing tobacco, and the muzzle of ice held his lips so rigidly—that he was unable to clear his chin when he expelled the juice. The result was a crystal beard of amber on his chin. If he fell, it would shatter, like glass into brittle fragments.

MAN 1: He didn't mind. It was the penalty tobacco-chewers paid up here.

NARRATOR 1: After several miles, the man came to the frozen Henderson Creek.

MAN 2: Ten miles from the forks.

NARRATOR 1: He looked at his watch.

MAN 3: Ten o'clock. He was making four miles an hour.

MAN 2: He would arrive at the forks at half-past twelve—and celebrate that event by eating his lunch there.

DOG: The dog dropped in again at his heels, with a tail drooping discouragement as the man swung along the creek-bed.

NARRATOR 3: The furrow of the old sled-trail was plainly visible, but a dozen inches of snow covered the marks of the last runners.

MAN 1: In a month no man had come up or down that silent creek.

NARRATOR 2: The man held steadily on. He was not much given to thinking.

NARRATOR 1: He had nothing to think about—save that he would eat lunch at the forks and that at six o'clock he would be in camp with the boys.

From *Readers Theatre for Middle School Boys: Investigating the Strange and Mysterious* by Ann N. Black. Westport, CT: Teacher Ideas Press. Copyright © 2008.

NARRATOR 2: Besides, there was nobody to talk to. Anyway, speech would have been impossible because of the ice muzzle on his mouth.

NARRATOR 1: So he continued monotonously to chew tobacco and increase the length of his amber beard.

NARRATOR 3: Once in a while the thought reiterated itself—that it was very cold.

MAN 1: He'd never experienced such cold.

MAN 3: He rubbed his cheek-bones and nose with the back of his mittened hand, now and then changing hands. The instant he stopped, his cheek-bones went numb, then the end of his nose—numb.

MAN 2: He was sure to frost his cheeks. (*Short laugh*) What were frosted cheeks? A bit painful, that was all. They were never serious.

NARRATOR 4: Empty as the man's mind was of thoughts, he was keenly observant of the changes in the creek and sharply noted where he placed his feet.

MAN 3: The creek was frozen clear to the bottom, but springs bubbled from the hillsides and ran along under the snow and on top of the ice of the creek.

MAN 2: These springs never froze. They were traps. They hid pools of water under the snow—snow that might be three feet deep.

MAN 1: Sometimes a skin of ice half an inch thick covered them—and in turn, the ice was covered by the snow.

MAN 2: If one broke through, he would keep on breaking through for a while, sometimes getting wet up to the waist.

NARRATOR 4: Once, coming around the bend, he shied in panic. He had felt the ice give under his feet and heard the crackle of the snow-hidden ice skin.

NARRATOR 3: To get his feet wet in such a temperature meant trouble and danger.

MAN 1: At the very least it meant delay.

MAN 2: He would be forced to stop and build a fire, and under its protection to bare his feet while he dried his socks and moccasins.

NARRATOR 4: In the course of the next two hours he came upon similar traps.

NARRATOR 3: Once he had a close call, and once, suspecting danger, he compelled the dog to go on in front.

SOUND A: (*Dog whines*)

DOG: The dog didn't want to go. It hung back until the man shoved it forward—then it went quickly—across the white, unbroken surface.

NARRATOR 3: Suddenly it broke through—floundered—then got to firmer footing.

DOG: It had wet its forefeet and legs, and almost immediately the water that clung to it, turned to ice. It made quick efforts to lick the ice off its legs. Then it dropped down in the snow and began to bite out the ice that had formed between the toes.

NARRATOR 1: This was a matter of instinct—to permit the ice to remain would mean sore feet. It did not know this. But the man knew.

NARRATOR 3: He removed the mitten from his right hand and helped tear out the ice particles. He did not expose his fingers more than a minute, and was astonished at the swift numbness that smote them. He pulled on the mitten hastily, and beat the hand savagely across his chest.

SOUND A: (*Beating of hands on body*)

NARRATOR 4: At twelve o'clock the day was at its brightest. Yet the sun was too far south on its winter journey to clear the horizon. At half-past twelve, to the minute, he arrived at the forks of the creek, pleased at his speed.

MAN 1: He would certainly be with the boys by six!

MAN 2: He unbuttoned his jacket and shirt and drew forth his lunch.

NARRATOR 1: In that brief moment, numbness laid hold of the exposed fingers.

NARRATOR 2: He did not put the mitten on. Instead, he struck the fingers a dozen sharp smashes against his leg. Then he sat down on a snow-covered log to eat. He had had no chance to take even a bite of biscuit.

NARRATOR 1: He returned his fingers to the mitten and bared the other hand for eating. He tried to take a mouthful, but the ice-muzzle prevented.

MAN 1: He had forgotten to build a fire and thaw out!

MAN 2: He chuckled at his foolishness—and as he chuckled, noted the numbness creeping into the exposed fingers.

MAN 3: Also, he noted that the stinging—which had first come to his toes when he sat down—was passing away. He wondered whether the toes were warm or numb. He moved them inside the moccasins and decided they were numb. He pulled the mitten on hurriedly and stood.

MAN 1: He was a bit frightened. He stamped up and down until the stinging returned to his feet. No mistake about it, it *was* cold.

MAN 2: He strode up and down, stamping his feet, and threshing his arms.

MAN 3: Then he got out matches and proceeded to make a fire.

NARRATOR 3: From the undergrowth he got his firewood, and working carefully from a small beginning, he soon had a roaring fire.

NARRATOR 4: He thawed the ice from his face and ate his biscuits.

SOUND A: (*A few contented dog sounds begin and continue through the next two speeches*)

DOG: The dog took satisfaction in the fire, stretching out close enough for warmth and far enough away to escape being singed.

NARRATOR 3; When the man finished, he filled his pipe and took his comfortable time over a smoke. Then he pulled on his mittens and took to the trail.

DOG: The dog was disappointed. This man did not know cold.

NARRATOR 1: But the dog knew; all its ancestry knew. But there was no intimacy between the dog and the man. One was the toil-slave of the other.

NARRATOR 2: The only caresses it had ever received were the caresses of the whip-lash and of harsh sounds that threatened the whip-lash.

DOG: It was not concerned with the welfare of the man; it was for its own sake that it yearned back toward the fire.

NARRATOR 3: But the man whistled, and spoke to it with the sound of whip-lashes, and the dog swung in at the man's heels and followed after.

MAN 1: And then it happened!

MAN 2: At a place where there were no signs—where the soft, unbroken snow seemed to advertise solidity beneath—the man broke through.

MAN 3: It was not deep, but he got wet halfway to his knees.

NARRATOR 2: He was angry, and cursed his luck aloud.

MAN 1: This would delay him an hour. He would have to build a fire and dry out his foot gear.

MAN 2: This was imperative at that low temperature—he knew that much.

NARRATOR 1: Tangled in the underbrush was a deposit of dry firewood and dry grasses. These served for the foundation and would prevent the young flame from drowning in the snow that it would otherwise melt.

NARRATOR 3: For the flame, he touched a match to a small shred of birch-bark that he took from his pocket. Then he fed the flame with wisps of dry grass and the tiniest of dry twigs. He worked slowly, carefully.

MAN 1: Keenly aware of his danger, he knew he must not fail.

SOUND B: (*Fire begins to crackle and continues intermittently*)

MAN 3: Gradually the flame grew stronger. He increased the size of the twigs.

MAN 2: Already all sensation had gone out of his feet.

MAN 1: To build the fire he had been forced to remove his mittens. (*Pause*) His fingers had quickly gone numb.

NARRATOR 4: His pace of four miles an hour had kept his blood pumping to the surface of his body and to all his extremities, but the instant he stopped, the blood ebbed away—into the recesses of his body.

MAN 1: His wet feet froze faster—his exposed fingers numbed faster.

MAN 2: Nose and cheeks were already freezing.

MAN 3: But he was safe. The fire was beginning to burn with strength!

MAN 2: He remembered the advice of the old-timer on Sulphur Creek: no man must travel alone in the Klondike after fifty below. He smiled.

MAN 1: He had had the accident. He was alone. He had saved himself.

MAN 3: All a man had to do was keep his head, and he was all right.

MAN 2: Any man who was a man could travel alone.

MAN 1: But—surprising how fast his cheeks and nose were freezing. And his fingers—lifeless in so short a time. He could scarcely make them move together to grip a twig. They seemed remote from his body.

MAN 3: But there was the fire—promising life with every dancing flame!

NARRATOR 3: He started to untie his moccasins. They were coated with ice. His thick socks were like sheaths of iron halfway to his knees—and the moccasin strings were like rods of steel twisted and knotted.

MAN 3: For a moment he tugged with his numb fingers. Then, realizing the folly of it, he drew his sheath-knife.

MAN 2: But before he could cut the strings—it happened!

MAN 1: It was his own fault or, rather, his mistake. He should not have built the fire under the spruce tree. He should have built it out in the open.

NARRATOR 2: The tree carried a weight of snow on its boughs. Then—high up in the tree, one bough capsized its load of snow. This fell on the boughs below, capsizing them—until it grew like an avalanche!

NARRATOR 1: Snow descended without warning upon the man and the fire—and the fire was blotted out.

SOUND B: (*Fire out*)

NARRATOR 1: The man was shocked—as though—

MAN 3: (*Slowly*) As though he'd heard his own sentence of death.

MAN 1: For a moment, he sat and stared at the spot where the fire had been.

From *Readers Theatre for Middle School Boys: Investigating the Strange and Mysterious* by Ann N. Black. Westport, CT: Teacher Ideas Press. Copyright © 2008.

MAN 2: Then he grew very calm. Perhaps the old-timer on Sulpher Creek was right. If he had a trail-mate, he would be in no danger now. The trail-mate could have built the fire.

MAN 3: Well, it was up to him to build the fire over again, and this time there must be no failure. Even if he succeeded, he would most likely lose some toes. His feet must be badly frozen by now.

NARRATOR 3: Such were his thoughts, but he did not sit and think them. He made a new foundation for a fire—this time in the open. He gathered dry grasses and tiny twigs, even collected larger branches to use later.

DOG: And all the while, the dog sat and watched him, for it looked upon him as the fire-provider, and the fire was slow in coming.

NARRATOR 4: When all was ready, the man reached in his pocket for a second piece of birch-bark. He knew it was there, but he could not feel it with his fingers. He could hear it rustling as he fumbled for it.

NARRATOR 3: Try as he would, he could not catch hold of it.

NARRATOR 1: And all the time he knew his feet were freezing. This thought tended to put him in a panic, but he fought against it and kept calm.

MAN 1: He pulled on his mittens with his teeth.

MAN 2: He threshed his arms back and forth—beat his hands against his sides.

DOG: And all the while, the dog sat in the snow—its wolf-brush of a tail curled warmly over its forefeet—its sharp wolf-ears pricked forward intently, as it watched the man, as he beat and threshed with his arms.

MAN 3: And the man envied the creature warm, secure in its natural covering.

MAN 2: After a time, he was aware of the first far-away signals of sensation in his beaten fingers—then a stinging ache.

NARRATOR 2: He stripped the mitten from his right hand and brought forth the birch-bark—and next his bunch of sulphur matches. But the cold had driven the life from his fingers, and in his effort to separate one match from the others, the whole bunch fell in the snow.

NARRATOR 4: He pulled the mitten on the right hand, then managed to get the bunch between the heels of his mittened hands and carried it to his mouth.

NARRATOR 3: With a violent effort, he opened his mouth. Ice crackled and snapped. He drew the lower jaw in, curled the upper lip out of the way, scraped the bunch with his upper teeth—and separated one match.

NARRATOR 4: The match dropped in his lap. He picked it up with his teeth, scratched it twenty times on his leg before it flared up.

NARRATOR 2: He held it with his teeth to the birch-bark—but the burning sulphur went up his nostrils and into his lungs, causing him to cough spasmodically. The match fell into the snow and went out.

NARRATOR 1: Suddenly, he bared both hands, caught the whole bunch of matches between the heels of his hands, and scratched the bunch on his leg.

SOUND B: (*Heavy scraping of match. Slight crackle of fire.*)

MAN 1: It flared into flame! Seventy sulphur matches at once! Keeping his head to one side from the fumes, he became aware of (*Pause*) sensation in his hand. His hand was burning! He could smell it.

MAN 2: When he could endure no more, he jerked his hands apart. The blazing matches fell sizzling into the snow.

From *Readers Theatre for Middle School Boys: Investigating the Strange and Mysterious* by Ann N. Black. Westport, CT: Teacher Ideas Press. Copyright © 2008.

MAN 3: But the birch-bark was alight! He began laying dry grasses and the tiniest twigs on the flame—lifting the fuel with the heels of his hands.

MAN 1: Small pieces of rotten wood and green moss clung to the twigs, and he bit them off as well as he could with his teeth.

NARRATOR 3: He cherished the flame carefully and awkwardly. It meant life, and it must not perish. Then—he began to shiver. He grew more awkward.

NARRATOR 1: A large green piece of moss fell squarely on the fire.

MAN 1: He tried to poke it out with his fingers—but he poked too far.

MAN 2: He tried to poke the grasses and the twigs together, but his shivering got away with him, and the twigs were hopelessly scattered.

MAN 3: Each twig gushed a puff of smoke—and went out.

SOUND B: (*Fire out*)

DOG: The fire-provider had failed.

NARRATOR 4: The man looked apathetically about him. His eyes chanced on the dog. And the sight of the dog put a wild idea into his head. He remembered the tale of a man, caught in a blizzard, who killed a steer and crawled inside the carcass—and so was saved.

NARRRATOR 3: But even though he struggled with the dog, he could not hold it—could not kill it. There was no way to do it with his helpless hands.

SOUND A: (*Dog yips briefly*)

DOG: The dog plunged wildly away, its tail between its legs. Snarling, it halted, and with ears pricked, surveyed the man curiously.

NARRATOR 1: The man looked down at his hands in order to locate them, and found them hanging on the ends of his arms—like weights.

 From *Readers Theatre for Middle School Boys: Investigating the Strange and Mysterious* by Ann N. Black. Westport, CT: Teacher Ideas Press. Copyright © 2008.

NARRATOR 2: The fear of death came to him. He realized it was no longer a mere matter of freezing his fingers and toes, or of losing his hands and feet.

MAN 1: It was a matter of life and death—with the chances against him.

MAN 2: Panicked, he turned and ran up the creek-bed along the old, dim trail.

DOG: The dog joined in behind and kept up with him.

MAN 3: He ran blindly—without intention—in fear such as he'd never known.

MAN 1: The running made him feel better. Maybe, if he ran on, his feet would thaw out, and if he ran far enough, he'd reach camp and the boys.

NARRATOR 3: His theory had one flaw in it. He lacked the endurance. He stumbled, tottered, crumpled up, and fell. When he tried to rise, he failed.

MAN 2: He must sit and rest. Then he would merely walk and keep going.

NARRATOR 4: He sat and regained his breath.

MAN 1: He was feeling quite warm and comfortable. He was not shivering, and it even seemed a warm glow had come to his chest and trunk.

MAN 2: And yet—when he touched his nose or cheeks, there was no sensation. (*Pause*) Running would not thaw them out.

MAN 3: Nor would it thaw out his hands and feet.

DOG: And all the time, the dog ran with him, at his heels. When he fell down a second time, it curled its tail over its forefeet and sat in front of him—facing him, curiously eager and intent.

NARRATOR 1: The warmth and security of the animal angered him, and he cursed it.

From *Readers Theatre for Middle School Boys: Investigating the Strange and Mysterious* by Ann N. Black. Westport, CT: Teacher Ideas Press. Copyright © 2008.

DOG: It flattened down its ears appeasingly.

NARRATOR 3: The shivering came more quickly upon the man. He was losing his battle with the frost. It was creeping into his body from all sides.

NARRATOR 2: The thought of it drove him on—but he ran no more than a hundred feet, when he staggered and pitched headlong. It was his last panic.

MAN 1: He sat up and entertained the idea of meeting death with dignity.

MAN 2: He'd been making a fool of himself—running around like a chicken with its head cut off—such was the simile that occurred to him.

MAN 3: He was bound to freeze anyway. He might as well take it decently.

NARRATOR 4: With this new-found peace of mind came the first glimmerings of drowsiness. Freezing was not so bad as people thought. There were lots worse ways to die.

NARRATOR 1: Then the man drowsed off into what seemed to him the most comfortable and satisfying sleep he had ever known.

DOG: The dog sat facing him and waiting.

NARRATOR 2: The brief day drew to a close in a long, slow twilight.

DOG: No signs of a fire to be made. Besides, never in the dog's experience had it known a man to sit like that in the snow and make no fire.

NARRATOR 3: As the twilight drew on, its eager yearning for the fire mastered it.

DOG: Lifting and shifting its feet, it whined softly, then flattened its ears in anticipation of being chidden by the man.

NARRATOR 4: But the man remained silent.

DOG: Later, the dog whined loudly.

SOUND A: (*Dog whines*)

DOG: And still later, it crept close to the man and caught the scent of death.

NARRATOR 1: This made the animal bristle and back away.

NARRATOR 2: A little longer it delayed—howling under the stars that leaped and danced and shone brightly in the cold sky.

DOG: Then it turned and trotted up the trail in the direction of the camp it knew—where there were other food-providers and fire-providers.

SOUNDS A, B: (*Sound of twigs breaking; match being struck.*)

ENTIRE CAST: (*Pause. Close folders. Bow heads.*)

From *Readers Theatre for Middle School Boys: Investigating the Strange and Mysterious* by Ann N. Black. Westport, CT: Teacher Ideas Press. Copyright © 2008.

A Gruesome End with "The Masque of the Red Death" by Edgar Allan Poe

The man casts a long shadow: Edgar Allan Poe, poet, philosopher of aesthetics, and one of the most dramatic storytellers of all time. He is a classic, and his work has been honored at home and abroad for nearly two hundred years.

Yet, Edgar Allan Poe was born and lived under another shadow—one of poverty and neglect. Orphaned at age two when his father disappeared and his mother died, Poe was taken in by foster parents. He never knew financial security. He never had the love of complete acceptance until he moved into his aunt's house with her and his young cousin, his grandmother, and his brother. This little ménage, though ill-fated, for a while provided Poe the stability he had longed for and needed.

His parents, traveling American actors, left him no visible legacy, but somehow they had willed him a sense of the dramatic that inspired him and eventually gave us unforgettable stories and ideas.

Born in 1809 Poe gradually emerged into a literary time that sparkled with the likes of Byron, Dickens, Thoreau, Longfellow, Hawthorne, and the Brontsë. Like them, Poe was different—bold and unusual. His poem "The Raven" made him a celebrity. His psychological twists, innovative detective stories, his rhythms, and his critiques of poetry, drama, songwriting, and even furniture further impressed the world.

In 1836 Poe married his thirteen-year-old cousin, Virginia—but he lost her a decade later to the ravages of that same tuberculosis that had claimed his mother and his brother. When Virginia died, Poe seemed to go off the deep end. Alcohol became a terrible problem. He became physically and emotionally ill. In 1849 he collapsed on the streets of Baltimore. Then, after lying comatose for days in a hospital, Poe died at age forty.

PRODUCTION NOTES

Edgar Allan Poe lived a short, painful life. Born near the beginning of the nineteenth century, he was surrounded by neglect, poverty, and the scourge of tuberculosis. Only forty years old when he died, Poe, nevertheless, left us a treasure trove of imaginative poems and stories unlike any others. "The Masque of the Red Death," ostensibly a horror story, suggests moral interpretations of universal concerns that are timeless.

The following script, while remaining faithful to Poe's words, also incorporates helpful interpretations of words and ideas that may be different and difficult for today's students.

This dramatic story offers an excellent opportunity for sound effects that students can easily manage—such as a muffled metronome for the ebony clock, footsteps, etc. Two students alone can handle these cues. Suggestions for them appear in the Sound Appendix. However, the performance will not suffer seriously if the sound effects are eliminated.

The whole class may be included in the reading. For example, in addition to the eight Readers and the Announcer, the remaining class members may participate as the Group, which responds to the dramatic action. This "choral Group" can be composed of any number of students—five, for example, as suggested here.

Reading stands for each of the eight Readers and the Announcer can be very helpful. In addition to these nine stands, one tall stool will be needed for the Announcer.

A minimum of eleven scripts will be required, plus one for the teacher. Five or more scripts will also be needed for the Group.

A Gruesome End with "The Masque of the Red Death" by Edgar Allan Poe

Sound A	Group	Sound B
X	X X X X X	X

Readers 2, 3, 4, 5	Readers 6, 7, 8
X X X X	X X X

Reader 1	Announcer
X	X

READER 1: Psst! (*Pause*) *Psst!*

READER 2: Psst! Listen up! Do you hear that?

READER 6: Hear what? I don't hear anything.

READER 7: Me neither. What's to hear?

From *Readers Theatre for Middle School Boys: Investigating the Strange and Mysterious* by Ann N. Black. Westport, CT: Teacher Ideas Press. Copyright © 2008.

READER 8: What do you think? Maybe their brains are rattlin' around.

READER 7: That sounds good to me!

GROUP: (*Soft intermittent series of low moans*)

READER 3: Ssssh!

READER 4: Listen up, everyone.

GROUP: (*Slightly louder moans.*)

READER 1: There! Do you hear that now?

GROUP: (*Low moans gradually fade away under next speech*)

READER 6: Oh, boy, do I! What's going on?

ANNOUNCER: Well, we thought you'd like to get in on the beginning—the gruesome beginning. I'm talking about a gruesome story.

READER 8: Hey, that could be interesting.

ANNOUNCER: Excellent. Are you ready?

READER 7: I'm ready—if it's really gruesome. I don't know about anyone else. But for me, just name it!

ANNOUNCER: Okay. This story is called—The Masque of the Red Death.

GROUP: (*Painfully. Softly.*) Ohhhhh. Blood. Blood! Blood.

READER 5: Oh, oh. They're back again.

READER 7: Well, we wanted gruesome.

READER 8: Hey, I think we're hooked. So, who wrote this gruesome story?

ANNOUNCER: Edgar Allan Poe, of course. Author of The Telltale Heart. That's another good one—and gruesome to the extreme. That's the story of a really sick person who kills his imagined enemy and cuts him up.

READER 8: In a million little pieces?

From *Readers Theatre for Middle School Boys: Investigating the Strange and Mysterious* by Ann N. Black. Westport, CT: Teacher Ideas Press. Copyright © 2008.

ANNOUNCER: Well, yes—maybe. I don't know. The point is, he buries all the pieces, and he thinks he's committed the perfect crime. But the heart goes on beating—beating.

SOUND A: (*Soft thumps match words in following line*)

ANNOUNCER: Thump. Thump. Thump. Then the police knock on the door.

SOUND B: (*A knocking on door*)

READER 6: Okay. That's scary.

ANNOUNCER: Enough? Well, how about Poe's The Fall of the House of Usher or The Raven?

READER 8: The Raven? That bird didn't scare me.

ANNOUNCER: No? Well, take a listen to what Poe invented in *this* story—about a plague—a dreadful sickness—a pestilence.

READER 7: I think we're ready now.

ANNOUNCER: Then let's begin—with Edgar Allan Poe's short, short story, The Masque of the Red Death. (*Sits*)

READER 1: The Red Death had long devastated the country. No pestilence had ever been so fatal or so hideous.

READER 2: Blood was its Avatar and its seal—the redness and the horror of blood.

READER 6: Avatar? What is that?

READER 7: Good word. Avatar means the plague—as if it had a human shape.

READER 6: I don't get it.

GROUP: (*Softly*) You will. You will! Listen!

READER 3: First there were sharp pains, and sudden dizziness, and then profuse bleeding at the pores, with—dissolution.

GROUP: Dissolve—then decay. Decay!

READER 4: The scarlet stains upon the body, and especially upon the face of the victim, meant the "pest-ban"—isolation—which shut him out from the aid and sympathy of his fellowmen.

READER 5: And the whole seizure, progress, and termination of the disease were the incidents of—half an hour.

READER 8: That's quick! Half an hour? Once you got it, you were dead!

READER 6: The people of that country must have been terrified.

READER 7: That country? Try kingdom—and people are dying everywhere!

READER 1: But the Prince, Prospero, was happy and dauntless and sagacious.

READER 8: *Sagacious.* What's this *sagacious*?

READER 6: Yes, yes—sagacious. Means wise.

READER 7: Oh, sure. We knew that.

READER 1: So—when the dominions of the prince were half depopulated, he summoned to his presence, a thousand hale and lighthearted friends from among the knights and dames of his court. Then with these friends, he retired to the deep seclusion of one of his castellated abbeys.

READER 8: Ah, *castellated*—fortified, like a castle, right?

READER 7: Yes, yes—will you hush!

READER 1: This abbey was an extensive and magnificent structure, the creation of the prince's own eccentric taste. A strong and lofty wall girdled it in with gates of iron. The courtiers, having entered, had brought along massive hammers, and they welded the bolts tight.

READER 2: They resolved to prohibit any means of *in*gress from without and *e*gress to any sudden impulses of despair or of frenzy from within. The abbey was amply provisioned. With such precautions, the courtiers might bid defiance to contagion.

READER 3: The external world could take care of itself.

READER 1: Exactly. In the meantime, it was folly to grieve, or to think.

READER 4: Indeed. The prince had provided all the appliances of pleasure. There were buffoons.

READER 6: Buffoons? You mean clowns?

READER 4: There were improvisatori.

READER 8: Improvisatori? Whew. Oh, improvise! Now you mean actors.

READER 4: (*Nods*) There were ballet-dancers, there were musicians, there was Beauty, there was wine.

READER 7: The prince had thought of everything—clowns, actors, dancers, musicians!

READER 5: All these and security were within. (*Pause*) Without—was the Red Death.

READER 8: So what happens? Sounds like a perfect setup to me. Party time, sooner or later.

READER 1: Toward the close of the fifth or sixth month of this seclusion, and while the pestilence raged most furiously abroad, Prince Prospero entertained his guests at a masked ball of the most unusual magnificence.

READER 3: But first let me tell of the rooms in which the masquerade was held. There were seven rooms—an imperial suite. It was a voluptuous scene—as what one might have expected from the prince's love of the bizarre.

READER 2: Seven rooms. The apartments were so irregularly disposed that one's vision embraced but little more than one at a time. There was a sharp turn at every twenty or thirty yards, and at each turn, another novel effect.

READER 4: To the right and left, in the middle of each wall, a tall and narrow Gothic window looked out upon a closed corridor.

READER 3: These windows were of stained glass—which varied in color according to the color of the decorations of each chamber.

READER 4: For example, that at the eastern extremity was hung in blue—and vividly blue were its windows.

READER 5: The second chamber was purple, and here the panes were purple.

READER 2: The third was green throughout, and so were the casements. The fourth was furnished and lighted with orange. The fifth, with white—the sixth with violet.

READER 3: The seventh apartment was closely shrouded in black velvet—tapestries that hung all over the ceiling and down the walls, falling in heavy folds upon a carpet of the same material and hue.

READER 1: In this chamber only, the color of the windows failed to correspond with the decorations. The panes here were scarlet—a deep blood color.

GROUP: (*Low, soft tones*) Scarlet. Scarlet. Deep, deep blood.

READER 1: Now in no one of the seven apartments was there any lamp or candelabrum. There was no light of any kind.

READER 6: This is beginning to be a little mysterious—spooky, even.

READER 7: Hush. I'm starting to like this!

READER 8: Be real! There had to be some kind of light.

READER 2: Ah! In the corridors, there stood, opposite to each window, a heavy tripod, bearing a brazier of fire that projected its rays through the tinted glass. Firelight glaringly illuminated the room.

READER 3: And thus were produced a multitude of gaudy and fantastic appearances.

READER 1: But in the western, or the black chamber, the effect of the firelight that streamed upon the dark hangings—through the blood-tinted panes—was ghastly in the extreme.

READER 3: The effect produced so wild a look upon the countenances of those who entered, few of the company were bold enough to set foot within its precincts at all.

READER 4: It was in this apartment, also, that there stood against the western wall, a gigantic clock of ebony.

SOUND A: (*Clock begins nine slow clangs*)

READER 8: Ebony? That's black. The whole room is black!

READER 7: Sssh. What about the clock? The clock must mean something.

READER 4: The sound of the clock was so peculiar that the musicians of the orchestra paused, momentarily, to listen to the sound.

READER 2: The waltzers perforce stopped their evolutions.

READER 5: The giddiest grew pale.

READER 2: The more aged and sedate passed their hands over their brows as if lost in thought—in confused reverie or meditation.

SOUND A: (*The clock strikes ninth time and stops*)

READER 3: (*Brief pause*) But when the echoes had fully ceased, a light laughter at once pervaded the assembly. The musicians looked at each other and smiled as if at their own nervousness and folly. They made whispering vows that the next chiming of the clock should produce in them no similar emotion.

READER 6: And then—and then. . . .

READER 1: After the lapse of sixty minutes (which embrace three thousand and six hundred seconds of the Time that flies), there came yet another chiming of the clock.

SOUND A: (*Clock again begins to strike, this time ten clangs. Then it stops.*)

READER 1: Then were the same discomfort and tremulousness and meditation as before.

READER 5: But in spite of these things, it was a gay and magnificent revel. Certainly, the tastes of the prince were peculiar—unusual. He had a fine eye for colors and effects, disregarding mere fashion.

READER 3: His plans were bold and fiery, and his conceptions glowed with barbaric luster. (*Pause*) But there are some who would have thought him mad.

READER 6: Mad? I can understand that all right.

READER 3: His followers felt he was not.

READER 4: It was necessary to hear and see and touch him to be sure that he was not—mad.

READER 1: And it was his own guiding taste which had given character to the masqueraders. Be sure—they were grotesque—delirious fancies, such as the madman fashions. There was much of the beautiful, much of the wicked, much of the bizarre, something of the terrible—and not a little of that which might have excited disgust.

READER 8: Disgust? I think we can relate to that!

READER 7: I'm into this! Use your imagination, can't you?

READER 2: To and fro in the seven chambers there stalked, in fact, a multitude of dreams. The dreams writhed in and about, taking on the colors of the rooms, and causing the wild music of the orchestra to seem as an echo of their steps.

READER 3: And anon strikes the ebony clock.

SOUND A: (*Muffled chimes of the clock begin. Clock will strike eleven times*)

READER 4: And then, for a moment, all is still, and all is silent. The dreams are stiff-frozen as they stand.

GROUP: (*Soft scattered whispers and soft nervous laughter*)

SOUND A: (*Clock finishes*)

READER 5: And now—again the music swells.

READER 4: And the dreams live, and writhe to and fro more merrily than ever.

READER 2: But to the chamber which lies most westwardly of the seven, there now none of the maskers venture, for the night is waning away; and there flows a ruddier light through the blood-colored panes.

READER 3: And the blackness of the sable drapery appalls; and to him whose foot falls upon the sable carpet, there comes, from the near clock of ebony, a muffled peal—solemnly emphatic.

SOUND B: (*Muffled bell rings three times*)

READER 2: But the other apartments were densely crowded, and in them beat feverishly the heart of life.

READER 4: And the revel went whirlingly on, until at length—

SOUND A: (*Clock begins to strike midnight*)

READER 4: There commenced the sounding of midnight upon the clock.

READER 3: And the music ceased.

READER 4: And the spinning and evolutions of the waltzers were quieted.

READER 5: And there was an uneasy cessation of all things, as before.

READER 8: So everything has stopped again. So what's happening?

READER 7: Sssh. (*Whispers*) The clock is striking midnight.

READER 1: And thus it happened—perhaps. Before the last echoes of the last chime had utterly sunk into silence, there were many individuals in the crowd who had found leisure to become aware of the presence of a Masked Figure—a figure which had arrested the attention of no single individual before.

READER 2: The rumor of this new presence having spread itself whisperingly around, there arose from the whole company a buzz, or murmur—expressive of disapproval and surprise—then, finally, of terror, of horror, and of disgust.

SOUND A: (*Last strikes of midnight*)

GROUP: Oh—oh—oh! (*Sharp intake of breath for collective gasp*)

READER 1: The figure in question had gone beyond the bounds of even the prince's ill-defined manners of behavior and dress.

GROUP: (*Fading*) Oh, oh, oh.

READER 1: There are chords in the hearts of even the most reckless which cannot be touched without emotion. Even with the utterly lost, to whom life and death are equally jests, there are matters of which no jest can be made.

READER 2: The Figure was tall and gaunt, and shrouded from head to foot in garments of the grave.

READER 3: The mask resembled the countenance of a stiffened corpse.

READER 8: I'm beginning to get the picture.

READER 7: It's scary—but wasn't that the idea for some of the masqueraders?

READER 4: All this might have been endured, if not approved by the mad revelers—but the mummer, the Figure in disguise, had gone so far as to assume the image of the Red Death.

READER 3: His vesture—his shroud—was dabbled in *blood*—and his broad brow, with all the features of the face, was besprinkled with the scarlet horror.

GROUP: (*Gasp of horror*)

READER 5: When the eyes of Prince Prospero fell upon this Spectral Image—which stalked to and fro among the waltzers—the prince was seen to be convulsed—in the first moment, with a strong shudder either of terror or distaste; but, in the next, his brow reddened with rage.

READER 2: "Who dares?" he demanded of the courtiers who stood near him—"who dares insult us with this blasphemous mockery? Seize him and unmask him—that we may know whom we have to hang at sunrise, from the battlements!"

READER 3: It was in the eastern or blue chamber in which stood the Prince Prospero as he uttered these words. They rang throughout the seven rooms loudly and clearly—for the prince was a bold and robust man, and the music had hushed at the waving of his hand.

READER 5: It was in the blue room where stood the prince, with a group of pale courtiers by his side. At first, as he spoke, there was a slight rushing movement of this group in the direction of the Intruder—who—at the moment, was also near at hand.

SOUND B: (*Slow, steady footsteps*)

READER 5: Now (*Slowly*) with deliberate and stately step, the Intruder made closer his approach to the prince.

READER 4: But—from a certain nameless awe with which the mad assumptions of the Mummer had inspired the whole party, no one put forth a hand to seize him.

READER 8: Nobody raised a hand? But he was splattered with blood!

GROUP: No. (*Pause*) No. (*Slowly whispering*) No—no one.

READER 4: Unimpeded, the Intruder passed within a yard of the prince.

READER 5: And, while the vast assembly—as if with one impulse—shrank from the centre of the room to the walls, he made his way uninterruptedly—

READER 3: But—with the same solemn and measured step which had distinguished him from the first.

READER 2: He made his way through the blue chamber to the purple—

READER 3: Through the purple to the green—

READER 4: Through the green to the orange—

READER 5: Through this again to the white—and even thence to the violet ere any decided movement had been made to arrest him.

READER 1: It was then, however, that the Prince Prospero, maddening with rage and the shame of his own momentary cowardice, rushed hurriedly through the six chambers, while none followed him on account of a deadly terror that had seized upon all!

READER 8: Clever prince. He's bound to save his people again.

READER 6: You think so? He seems to have told everyone else what to do—to unmask the fiend—so they can hang him at sunrise!

READER 1: The prince bore aloft a drawn dagger, and had approached, in rapid impetuosity, to within three or four feet of the retreating Figure—when the spectral vision, having obtained the very end of the velvet apartment—turned suddenly and confronted his pursuer.

READER 2: There was a sharp cry!

From *Readers Theatre for Middle School Boys: Investigating the Strange and Mysterious* by Ann N. Black. Westport, CT: Teacher Ideas Press. Copyright © 2008.

READER 3: The dagger dropped, gleaming, upon the sable carpet—upon which, instantly afterwards—fell prostrate in death the Prince Prospero.

GROUP: Aah! Aah!

READER 4: Summoning the wild courage of despair, a throng of revelers at once threw themselves into the black apartment.

READER 3: Seizing the Mummer, whose tall figure stood erect and motionless within the shadow of the ebony clock, they gasped in unutterable horror!

READER 2: They found the grave-clothing and the corpselike mask, which they had handled with so violent a rudeness, uninhabited by any tangible form.

GROUP: Empty. Empty. No—one—there.

READER 8: You mean—under that shroud for the dead—

READER 7: No one was there. Nothing!

READER 1: (*Slow. Deliberate.*) And now was acknowledged the presence of the Red Death. He had come like a thief in the night. And one by one, dropped the revelers in the blood-bedewed halls of their revel, and died—each in the despairing posture of his fall.

GROUP: Oh—oh—oh!

READER 2: And the life of the ebony clock went out with the last life.

SOUND A: (*One last feeble strike of the clock*)

SOUND B: (*Metallic spring collapses*)

READER 3: And the flames of the tripods expired.

GROUP: (*Soft exhaling*)

READER 1: And Darkness and Decay and the Red Death held illimitable dominion over all.

From *Readers Theatre for Middle School Boys: Investigating the Strange and Mysterious* by Ann N. Black. Westport, CT: Teacher Ideas Press. Copyright © 2008.

ANNOUNCER: (*Stands*) The prince was thought to be sagacious—wise. But selfishly, stupidly, he and his so-called friends thought they could protect themselves from evil—by running away. They enjoyed themselves—never mind the rest of the world.

READER 5: Then the Red Death. He had come like a thief in the night.

READER 4: One by one the revelers dropped in the blood-bedewed halls.

READER 3: And the life of the ebony clock went out.

READER 2: And the flames of the tripod expired.

READER 1: And Darkness and Decay and the Red Death had triumphed.

ANNOUNCER: Pleasant dreams! Now—be sure to check out another wild dream or two—straight from the pen of Edgar Allan Poe—that master of the macabre. Invite him in. Let him stir your imagination with his stories of death and revenge—or the plague. Gruesome? But fascinating! Happy dreams—of black, black masks and bright red blood! (*Laughs*)

ALL READERS: (*Close books. Scary whisper.*) The Red Death waits for no one!

From *Readers Theatre for Middle School Boys: Investigating the Strange and Mysterious* by Ann N. Black. Westport, CT: Teacher Ideas Press. Copyright © 2008.

H. G. Wells in "The Country of the Blind"

H. G. Wells—a man of many parts—at once prolific, provocative, and prophetic. He was a man whose bibliography lists nearly three thousand entries of novels, short stories, essays, reviews, and lectures. He was a writer who challenged the status quo of Victorian England with his then-radical attitudes toward society, and women in particular. He was a man and an author who envisioned a better world, a Utopia. Time and time again, his imaginative narratives of these worlds have come alive for us.

Wells was born ordinary. The town was Bromley, near London. His parents—lower-middle-class. His physical attributes—modest. He was short and tubby, with small feet and a prominent forehead. But his intelligence and his imagination were extraordinary. His birth in 1866 led us into new worlds.

As the 1800s rolled into a new century, the wonders of scientific experiments invigorated all thinking men and women, certainly H. G. Wells. He foresaw tank warfare, aerial warfare, television, and space travel, and he used these far-fetched notions in his fantasies, such as *The Time Machine* and *The War of the Worlds.*

Wells married twice and had three sons, one out of wedlock by the writer Rebecca West. Nathaniel West, born of these two literary parents, also became a writer. In many ways, H. G. Wells was a bon vivant. He traveled widely and enjoyed the company and arguments of literary men and colleagues such as George Bernard Shaw, Henry James, and Joseph Conrad.

Wells was an educator at heart, seeking truth and furthering the study of science and history. His life and his works echo the words of Prospero, for they were, indeed, "such stuff as dreams are made of." Wells, the man, died in 1946, but his dreams—never.

PRODUCTION NOTES

H. G. Wells, who could thrill us with the unthinkable such as invisible men and visible Martians, infused his fantasies with scientific what-ifs. At the same time, he fires our imaginations and pricks our consciousness with his concerns for humanity. In "The Country of the Blind," we see a poignant, ultimately chilling picture of one man who tries to cope with a fantasy world long hidden in the Andes Mountains.

A subtle tone pervades this story. Reason and logic seem to hold sway. Sound effects of muffled bells, flickering birdcalls, and quiet drumbeats will add to the mysterious setting of this fantasy. The Sound Appendix lists suggestions for making and executing these sounds.

The script calls for a speaking cast of fifteen and a sound crew of two. The original story, basically narrated by one man, has little dialogue. To aid in the dramatic presentation of the story, four Narrators and two Readers handle the narrative threads. In general, the lines for the Readers are undiluted from the text. The Narrators, on the other hand, condense the text somewhat in order to explain the action from time to time. Following this plan of adaptation, the protagonist, Nunez, has been given a "shadow," ergo Nunez 1 and Nunez 2. With this arrangement, more readers can participate in the reading with less stress for all.

It is possible to reduce the cast size. One or two readers can handle all the Narrator lines. One person can handle all the lines for Readers 1 and 2. Nunez can lose his shadow and read the lines for both Nunez 1 and 2.

A full cast and crew will require seventeen scripts, plus one for the teacher.

H. G. Wells in "The Country of the Blind"

Sound 1		Man 2	Man 3		Sound 2
X		X	X		X
	Medina-sarote		Old Yacob; Doctor		
	X		X X		
Narrators1–4; Readers 1 & 2			Nunez 1 & 2		Pedro, Correa, Man 1
X X X X X			X X		X X X

NARRATOR 1: Maybe you'll think this story's true. Maybe not. Perhaps, a Could Be?

NARRATOR 2: Oh, I see. A fairy tale—or a myth—or some famous legend?

SOUND 1: (*Muffled bells begin to jangle off and on through next ten speeches*)

From *Readers Theatre for Middle School Boys: Investigating the Strange and Mysterious* by Ann N. Black. Westport, CT: Teacher Ideas Press. Copyright © 2008.

NARRATOR 1: Wrong! You're wrong on all three counts. H. G. Wells himself dreamed up this story. You know this writer. *The Time Machine. The Invisible Man.* How about *The War of the Worlds*? That H. G. Wells!

NARRATOR 2: Oh. *Those* books! We're talking spooky and scary. Out of this world!

NARRATOR 3: Well, believe me—The Country of the Blind is all that and more!

NARRATOR 2: The worlds of H. G. Wells aren't real. So, how does he think them up?

NARRATOR 1: Think! You hit the nail on the head! Wells was a thinker—with a great imagination. But who knows what inspires a storyteller? A map? A picture? A vision? Maybe an old proverb, or a sound—like bells?

NARRATOR 2: Aw, he was just an ordinary Englishman—writing books and stuff.

SOUND 2: (*Hands begin low, slow rhythmic beat on small drum*)

NARRATOR 1: Of course! But in his imagination—in this story, Wells travels. He becomes Nunez, a mountaineer from Ecuador—a guide for a group of Englishmen who want to climb Chimborazo, the tallest and most dangerous peak of the Andes Mountains.

NARRATOR 3: Remember, the Andes are mountains tormented by storms and volcanoes—volcanoes that can erupt and kill or hide all life.

NARRATOR 4: Here, in the Andes, lies a mysterious hidden valley where people live in a lost country—a forgotten country—The Country of the Blind.

SOUNDS 1, 2: (*Bells and drum fade away*)

NARRATOR 1: The little party had climbed all the way to the very foot of the last, greatest precipice. The men prepared to spend the night there, when they discovered suddenly that their guide Nunez had disappeared.

READER 1: They shouted, and there was no reply; shouted and whistled!

READER 2: As the morning broke, they saw the traces of his fall. He had slipped towards the unknown side of the mountain—straight to the edge of a frightful precipice. Beyond that—everything was hidden.

NARRATOR 2: Oh, boy. So much for the guide. Nunez—he's a goner, right?

READER 1: No. He survived! He fell a thousand feet in a cloud of snow—whirled, stunned, and insensible. But without a bone broken.

READER 2: His knife was gone. His hat was lost, and his ice axe had disappeared.

NARRATOR 4: Below, he saw a ledge strewn with rocks and dirt. After his struggles to reach it, he dropped down exhausted, and fell instantly asleep.

SOUND 1: (*Sound of little birds chirping*)

NARRATOR 1: He was awakened by the singing of birds far below.

NARRATOR 3: He looked about him. Surrounded by walls of rock, he spied (*Excited*) a gully down which a man might venture—if he were desperate.

NARRATOR 1: Surprisingly, the climb down was not too hard, and it brought him to a steep slope of trees—and further on, green meadows with a cluster of stone huts. He struggled on towards them.

NARRATOR 2: Oh, how lucky—to a nice little mountain village.

READER 2: The houses were very strange to his eyes, and indeed the whole aspect of the valley queer and unfamiliar.

NUNEZ 1: The greater part was lush green meadow, starred with many beautiful flowers, irrigated with

NUNEZ 2: And on the higher slopes, flocks of llamas cropped the scanty grasses.

NUNEZ 1: Paths, paved with black and white stones, and each with a curious little curb at the side, ran hither and thither in an orderly manner.

READER 1: The houses were quite unlike the casual higgledy-piggledy agglomeration of mountain villages he knew.

READER 2: They stood in a continuous row on either side of a central street of astonishing cleanness. Here and there each façade was pierced by a door—but not one single window.

NUNEZ 1: They were smeared with a plaster that was sometimes grey, sometimes drab, sometimes slate-colored or brown—parti-colored.

NUNEZ 2: It was the sight of this wild plastering that first brought the word *blind* into the thoughts of Nunez.

NUNEZ 1: The good man who did that must have been blind as a bat!

NARRATOR 3: Still climbing downward, he could see men and women resting on piles of grass, as if taking a siesta—and children, too, near the village.

READER 1: Then, nearer at hand, three men, dressed in llama cloth and leather, carrying pails on yokes, followed one another in single file, walking slowly and yawning—like men who have been up all night.

NUNEZ 2: Nunez stood forward, conspicuously, and gave vent to a mighty shout.

READER 2: The three men stopped—moved their heads as though looking about them. Nunez waved wildly, but the men did not appear to see him.

NUNEZ 2: Nunez yelled again and again as he gestured ineffectually.

NUNEZ 1: Blind! The fools must be blind!

READER 1: After much shouting and wrath, Nunez crossed the stream by a little bridge—came through a gate in the wall, and approached them.

READER 2: They stood close together—like men a little afraid. He could see their eyelids closed and sunken—as though the very eyeballs beneath had shrunken away. There was an expression of near awe on their faces. Nunez was sure that they were blind. Not only that, this was—

NUNEZ 1: This was the Country of the Blind—of which the legends told.

NUNEZ 2: All the old stories of the lost valley and the Country of the Blind had come back to his mind, and through his thoughts ran this old proverb, like a refrain:

NUNEZ 1: (*Slowly*) In the Country of the Blind, the One-eyed Man is King. (*Stronger*) In the Country of the Blind, the One-eyed Man is King.

NUNEZ 2: Then a man spoke to him in hardly recognizable Spanish.

CORREA: A man—a man it is—a man or a spirit—coming down from the rocks.

MAN 1: Where does he come from, brother Pedro?

PEDRO: Down out of the rocks.

NUNEZ 1: Over the mountains I come—out of the country beyond there—where men can see. From near Bogota—where there are a hundred thousands of people—and where the city passes out of sight.

From *Readers Theatre for Middle School Boys: Investigating the Strange and Mysterious* by Ann N. Black. Westport, CT: Teacher Ideas Press. Copyright © 2008.

PEDRO: Sight? Sight?

MAN 1: Come hither!

NARRATOR 1: The men moved towards him—their hands outstretched, their fingers spread out. Silently, they grabbed him and held him tight.

NARRATOR 2: I know—they want to examine him!

NUNEZ 2: With a finger in his eyes, Nunez cried out!

NUNEZ 1: Carefully! Carefully!

PEDRO: A strange creature, Correa. Feel the coarseness of his hair. Like a llama's hair.

CORREA: Rough he is as the rocks that begot him. Perhaps he will grow finer.

NUNEZ 1: Carefully! Carefully!

MAN 1: He speaks. Certainly he is a man. Feel his coat, too. Rough! Ugh!

PEDRO: Let us lead him to the elders.

CORREA: Shout first—lest the children be afraid. This is a marvelous occasion.

READER 1: And so they shouted, and Pedro took Nunez by the hand to lead him to the houses. Nunez drew his hand away.

NUNEZ 1: I can see. I can see!

CORREA: See? See?

NUNEZ 1: Yes, see.

NUNEZ 2: Nunez turned toward Correa, but he stumbled against Pedro's pail.

MAN 1: His senses are still imperfect. He stumbles, and talks unmeaning words. Lead him by the hand.

NUNEZ 1: (*Laughs*) As you will!

NUNEZ 2: It seemed they knew nothing of sight. Well, all in good time he would teach them.

READER 1: He heard people shouting, and saw a number of figures gathering together in the middle roadway of the village.

READER 2: His three guides kept close to him, and said again and again—"A wild man out of the rocks."

NUNEZ 1: No! Bogota. Bogota! Over the mountain crests.

PEDRO: A wild man—using wild words. Did you hear that? Bogota! His mind has hardly formed yet. He has only the beginnings of speech. We must bring him to the elders.

SOUND 2: (*Low, slow, ominous beating on drum*)

READER 2: And they thrust him suddenly through a doorway into a room as black as pitch, save at the end there faintly glowed a fire.

READER 1: The voice of an older man began to question him, and Nunez found himself trying to explain the great world out of which he had fallen—the sky and mountains and such-like marvels—to these elders who sat in darkness in the Country of the Blind.

SOUND 2: (*Drumming fades out*)

NUNEZ 1: They would believe and understand nothing. Much of their imagination had shriveled with their eyes. They explained their past.

PEDRO: Into the valley had first come llamas, then men, and at last, angels, whom one could hear singing and making fluttering sounds, but whom no one could touch at all.

NARRATOR 2: Of course—those were the birds.

READER 2: The elder described how time had been divided into the warm and the cold—the blind equivalents of night and day.

PEDRO: Nunez must have been specially created to learn and serve the wisdom we have acquired.

CORREA: For all his stumbling, he must have courage and do his best to learn.

READER 1: Then they brought him llama's milk and rough, salted bread, and led him to a lonely place to eat, out of their hearing, and to slumber.

NUNEZ 2: But Nunez slumbered not at all. Instead, he sat up thinking. Thinking.

NUNEZ 1: Unformed! No senses! Little they know they've been insulting their Heaven-sent King and master! I see I must bring them to reason.

NUNEZ 2: He was still thinking when the sun set—when the glow upon the snow-fields and glaciers was the most beautiful thing he'd ever seen.

NUNEZ 1: He thanked God from the bottom of his heart that the power of sight had been given to him.

SOUND 1: (*Bells jangle softly, briefly*)

NUNEZ 2: Then he heard a voice calling him from out of the village.

MAN 2: Yaho there, Bogota! Come hither!

NUNEZ 2: He stood up, smiling. He would show these people once and for all what sight would do. (*Cleverly*) They would seek, but not find him.

MAN 2: You move not, Bogota.

NUNEZ 2: He made two stealthy steps aside from the path.

MAN 2: Trample not on the grass, Bogota; that is not allowed.

READER 1: The owner of the voice came running up the path toward him.

NUNEZ 2: He stepped back into the pathway.

NUNEZ 1: Here I am!

MAN 2: Why did you not come when I called you? Must you be led like a child? Cannot you hear the path as you walk?

NUNEZ 1: (*Laughs*) I can see it!

MAN 2: There is no such word as *see*. Cease this folly and follow the sound of my feet.

NUNEZ 1: My time will come!

MAN 2: You'll learn. There is much to learn in the world.

NUNEZ 1: Has no one told you—In the Country of the Blind the One-Eyed Man is King?

MAN 2: (*Short, scornful laugh*) What is blind?

NARRATOR 1: But as the days went on, the King of the Blind was still clumsy and useless among his subjects, and he could not help but marvel at them.

NARRATOR 3: It was their senses. They could hear and judge the slightest gesture—even distances away. They could hear the very beating of his heart.

NARRATOR 1: Unable to read expressions, they changed the tones of their voice and used touch instead of gestures.

NARRATOR 2: What about their sense of smell?

NARRATOR 3. Fine! They could distinguish individual smells as readily as a dog can.

NUNEZ 2: He tried on several occasions to tell them of sight.

NUNEZ 1: Look here, you people. There are things you do not understand in me.

NUNEZ 2: And he did his best to tell them what it was to see.

NARRATOR 3: Nunez noticed a young girl among his listeners. Her eyelids seemed different—not as red or sunken—almost as if she was hiding eyes.

NARRATOR 2: Oh, oh. Something's going on here!

From *Readers Theatre for Middle School Boys: Investigating the Strange and Mysterious* by Ann N. Black. Westport, CT: Teacher Ideas Press. Copyright © 2008.

NARRATOR 4: He wanted to persuade about sight. So he went on describing the mountains, the sky, and the sunrise.

READER 1: They told him there were indeed no mountains at all—that the end of the rocks where the llamas grazed was indeed the end of the world; thence sprang a cavernous roof of the universe from which the dew and avalanches sprang.

READER 2: He maintained the world had neither end nor roof, as they supposed.

READER 1: They said his thoughts were wicked!

NARRATOR 1: That did it! He wanted to pick up a spade and smite one or two of them to earth. In combat, he would show the advantage of eyes!

NARRATOR 3: He actually seized his spade—then he discovered a new thing about himself: It was impossible for him to hit a blind man in cold blood.

MAN 3: Put that spade down!

READER 1: He thrust one man against a house wall, and fled past him and out of the village, leaving a track of trampled grass behind his feet.

READER 2: He felt something of the buoyancy that comes to all men in the beginning of a fight—but with more complexity. He began to realize you cannot fight happily with creatures who stand upon a different mental basis to yourself.

NARRATOR 1: Then, a wide line of men armed with spades and sticks, began advancing toward him. They spoke to one another, stopped, sniffed the air—and listened. He watched—and waited, with his spade.

NUNEZ 1: Should he charge them? The pulse in his ears ran into the rhythm of—In the Country of the Blind the One-Eyed Man is King.

NUNEZ 2: Should he charge them?

READER 1: He looked back at the high and unclimbable wall, pierced with many little doors, and he looked at the approaching line of seekers.

NUNEZ 1: Should he charge them?

MAN 2: Bogota! Bogota! Where are you?

NUNEZ 2: He gripped his spade still tighter and advanced. They converged upon him. (*Low*) I'll hit them if they touch me! By Heaven, I will. I'll hit!

NUNEZ 1: Look here, I'm going to do what I like in this valley! Do you hear? I'm going to do what I like and go where I like.

NARRATOR 4: They were moving in upon him quickly, groping, yet moving rapidly.

NARRATOR 2: Like playing blind man's bluff with everyone blindfolded, except one.

MAN 3: Get hold of him!

NUNEZ 1: You don't understand! You are blind and I can see. Leave me alone!

NUNEZ 2: He began to run—not knowing clearly where to run.

READER 1: He ran from the nearest blind man, because it was a horror to hit him. He made a dash for where a gap in the wall was wide—a dash to escape from their closing ranks.

NUNEZ 2: And then he saw he would be caught! Swish! The spade had struck.

NUNEZ 1: The man was down with a yell of pain—and he was through the wall!

READER 2: He lay down, sobbing for breath. (*Pause*) He stayed outside the wall of the valley of the blind for two nights and days without food or shelter, often meditating upon that proverb.

From *Readers Theatre for Middle School Boys: Investigating the Strange and Mysterious* by Ann N. Black. Westport, CT: Teacher Ideas Press. Copyright © 2008.

NUNEZ 1: (*Bitter*) Ha! In the Country of the Blind the One-Eyed Man is King!

NARRATOR 3: He knew he could not fight and conquer these people. He had no weapons—could get none. Besides, the infection of civilization from Bogotá had affected him. He could not find it in himself to assassinate a blind man.

READER 1: On the second day, fear came to him and fits of shivering. He crawled down to the wall, crawled along the stream, shouting. Two men came.

NUNEZ 1: I was mad! But I was only newly made.

NUNEZ 2: He told them he was wiser now, and repented of all he had done. Then he wept without intention, for he was very weak and ill now.

MAN 3: That was better. Do you still think you can *see*?

NUNEZ 1: No. That was folly. The word means nothing. Less than nothing!

MAN 4: So, then, tell us what is overhead.

NUNEZ 1: There is a roof above the world—of rock—and very, very smooth. So smooth—so beautifully smooth. . . .

NARRATOR 4: He broke down with hysterical tears.

NUNEZ 1: Before you ask me any more, give me some food, or I shall die!

NARRATOR 1: Instead of his expected punishment, the people regarded his rebellion as just one more proof of his general idiocy and inferiority.

READER 2: So Nunez became a citizen of the Country of the Blind, and the world beyond the mountains became more and more remote and unreal.

NARRATOR 3: There was Old Yacob, his master, and Pedro, Old Yacob's nephew—and Medina-sarote, the youngest daughter of Old Yacob.

NARRATOR 2: Oh, the pretty girl who listened to him—the girl he wants to marry.

READER 2: Nunez thought that if he could win her in marriage, he would be resigned to live in the valley the rest of his days. But there was great opposition to the marriage of Medina-sarote and Nunez.

READER 1: They held him as a being apart—an idiot—an incompetent thing.

READER 2: It would bring discredit on them all! It would corrupt the race!

NARRATOR 4: Old Yacob grieved when Medina-sarote wept on his shoulder.

OLD YACOB: You see, my dear, he's an idiot. He has delusions. He can't do anything right.

MEDINA: But he's better than he was. And he's strong, dear father, and kind—stronger and kinder than any other man in the world.

OLD YACOB: (*Nods*) He's better than he was. Very likely, some day, we shall find him as sane as ourselves.

NARRATOR 4: Old Yacob, distressed for his daughter, sought help from the council.

READER 1: One of the elders, who thought deeply, had an idea. He was a great doctor among these people, and the idea of curing Nunez of his peculiarities appealed to him.

DOCTOR: I have examined Nunez, and the case is clearer to me. I think very probably he might be cured.

OLD YACOB: This is what I've always hoped.

DOCTOR: His brain is affected.

OLD YACOB: (*Nods*) Ah, yes. (*Nods again*)

From *Readers Theatre for Middle School Boys: Investigating the Strange and Mysterious* by Ann N. Black. Westport, CT: Teacher Ideas Press. Copyright © 2008.

DOCTOR: Now, *what* affects it? *This*! These queer things that are called eyes, which exist to make an agreeable depression in the face, are diseased.

OLD YACOB: Diseased? Diseased? The eyes of Nunez?

DOCTOR: (*Nods*) Diseased in such a way as to affect his brain. They are greatly distended. He has eyelashes, and his eyelids move, and consequently his brain is in a state of constant irritation and distraction.

OLD YACOB: Yes? Yes, yes? So?

DOCTOR: I think I may say with reasonable certainty that, in order to cure him complete, all that we need to do is a simple and easy surgical operation—namely to remove these irritant bodies.

OLD YACOB: And then he will be sane?

DOCTOR: Then he will be perfectly sane, and a quite admirable citizen.

OLD YACOB: Thank Heaven for science! I must tell Nunez at once!

NARRATOR 1: But when Nunez received this good news, his response seemed cold and disappointing to Old Yacob. It was Medina-sarote who persuaded Nunez to face the blind surgeons. And yet, Nunez pleaded with her.

NUNEZ 1: You do not want me to lose my gift of sight? My world is sight!

NUNEZ 2: There are the beautiful things—the flowers, the lichens amidst the rocks, the far sky with its drifting dawn of clouds, the sunsets and the stars. And there is you. For you alone it is good to have sight.

NUNEZ 1: It is these eyes of mine that these idiots seek. I must come under that roof of rock and stone and darkness—that horrible roof under which your imaginations stoop? No! You would not have me do that?

 From *Readers Theatre for Middle School Boys: Investigating the Strange and Mysterious* by Ann N. Black. Westport, CT: Teacher Ideas Press. Copyright © 2008.

SOUND 2: (*Hands begin slow, low beating on the small drum*)

MEDINA: I wish—I wish sometimes you would not talk like that. I know it's pretty—it's your imagination. I love it, but now. . . .

NUNEZ 1: You mean—you think—I should be better, better perhaps. . . .

NUNEZ 2: He was realizing things very swiftly, and he felt anger at the dull course of fate, but sympathy and pity for her lack of understanding.

NUNEZ 1: Medina-sarote—if I were to consent to this?

MEDINA: Oh, if you would! If only you would!

NUNEZ: Then—tomorrow I shall see no more.

MEDINA: Oh, Nunez—they will hurt you a little, but I swear that I'll repay you.

NARRATOR 1: He looked at her face for the last time. Then, in silence, turned away.

SOUNDS 1, 2: (*Drumming stops. Slow footsteps begin. Muffled bells jangle.*)

READER 2: He walked away. He had fully meant to go to a lonely place where the meadows were beautiful with white narcissus, and there remain until the hour of his sacrifice should come.

READER 1: But as he walked, he lifted up his eyes and saw the morning—like an angel in golden armour marching down the steep slopes.

SOUND 1: (*Footsteps stop*)

READER 2: And it seemed, before all this splendour, that he and this blind world in the valley—Medina-sarote and all—were no more than a pit of sin.

SOUNDS 1: (*Bells stop*)

From *Readers Theatre for Middle School Boys: Investigating the Strange and Mysterious* by Ann N. Black. Westport, CT: Teacher Ideas Press. Copyright © 2008.

READER 1. He did not turn aside, as he had meant to do. He went on—passed through the encircling wall and out upon the rocks.

NARRATOR 3: And his eyes were on the beauty of the sunlit ice and snow, and his imagination soared to the things beyond he was now to resign forever.

NARRATOR 4: He thought of that great free world he was parted from, and he had a vision of further slopes—distance beyond distance—to Bogota.

NARRATOR 3: Of the river journey from great Bogota to the limitless sea beyond—

READER 2: There, unpent by mountains, one saw the sky, not as a disc, but as an arch of immeasurable blue in which circling stars were floating.

NARRATOR 1: His eyes began to scrutinize the great curtain of the mountains.

NUNEZ 1: (*Thoughtfully*) For example—if one went so—up that gully, so—one might come out among those pines above the gorge.

NUNEZ 2: Then perhaps a climb to the precipice below the snow—or another way farther to the east. Then out upon the snow, halfway to the crest.

NARRATOR 4: For a moment, he glanced back at the village, but then he turned clear round. Now he regarded it with folded arms.

NUNEZ 1: He thought of Medina-sarote, and she had become small and remote.

READER 1: He turned again towards the mountain—and he began his climb.

NARRATOR 1: When sunset came, he was no longer climbing, but he was far and high. His clothes were torn, his limbs were blood-stained, he was bruised in many places, but as he lay down, a smile was on his face.

 From *Readers Theatre for Middle School Boys: Investigating the Strange and Mysterious* by Ann N. Black. Westport, CT: Teacher Ideas Press. Copyright © 2008.

READER 1: And the little things in the rocks near at hand were drenched with beauty—green mineral, orange lichen, a flash of crystal.

NUNEZ 2: But he heeded these things no longer, but lay quite still there, smiling as if he were content now merely to have escaped from the valley of the Blind, in which he had thought to be King.

NUNEZ 1: And the glow of the sunset passed, and the night came, and still he lay there, under the cold, clear stars.

NARRATOR 2: (*After a brief pause*) Oh, I see—I think I see. Sometimes I think we fall into a kind of country of the blind. But you are right. H. G. Wells was a real thinker—with some imagination! What else did he write? I bet a lot! Out of this world, huh? Okay—next time!

From *Readers Theatre for Middle School Boys: Investigating the Strange and Mysterious* by Ann N. Black. Westport, CT: Teacher Ideas Press. Copyright © 2008.

Sound Appendix

Incorporating sound effects into readers' theatre scripts should heighten the intent and the effect of the literature. At the same time, adding a small sound-effects crew to the cast of oral readers increases the number of students actively engaged in the performance. Luckily, the exuberant, inventive nature of middle school boys makes them particularly creative and resourceful in developing and executing sound effects.

Viola Spolin, teacher, director, and leading proponent of improvisational techniques for the theatre, describes one of her exercises where "sound effects are not to be mechanically reproduced but are to be done vocally by the players. . . . Almost invariably, one or more students will delight in this exercise and will develop skills in sound effects to such an extent that mechanical aids will be almost unnecessary" (Viola Spolin, *Improvisation for the Theater* [Northwestern: Northwestern University Press, 1963], 205).

Students who begin to listen carefully to all kinds of sounds will develop their own techniques for reproducing mechanical sounds. For example, bird cries, wind sighs, clocks ticking, even doors opening can all be produced vocally. Standing in place, students can use their bodies to imitate the sounds of a horse galloping, footsteps running, a heart thumping. Common, everyday articles can provide other sounds. A light scrape of sandpaper says a match is struck. The slow crinkle of cellophane suggests a fire burning. Beanbags thud as rats. Clatter of pennies can represent a ransom, a wish fulfilled, or the payment for a piper. The students are inventive, and their sounds become real.

Being a member of the sound-effects crew is serious business—and the students will discover it's fun!

The list below identifies the sounds suggested for each of the scripts represented:

Browning, Robert: from *The Pied Piper of Hamelin*

Book slams

Rat sounds: squeaking and scurrying

Rat bodies fall into water

Knock on wood

Door opens and closes

Flute (or recorder, simple sound)

Water splashes

Coins

Gavel pounding

Patter of little feet

Rocks scraping

Doyle, Sir Arthur Conan, from "The Adventure of the Speckled Band"

Wind

Rain

Metal is tapped, clangs and bangs

Door: knocking, door opens, closes, squeaks, slams

Low whistle

Wildlife sounds: bird, cat-like, baboon

Clock strikes

Steam hissing

Finley, M. P., from Mary Peace Finley Spells Danger in *White Grizzly*

Whistling

Dog barks, whimpers, yelps; puppy mewlings

Twigs snapping

Harmonica tune

Door opens

Dinner table sounds (dishes, silverware)

Bell tolls

Whistle blows

Bear growls

Gawain-poet, from *Sir Gawain and the Green Knight*

Horse stomping; galloping

Bells jingle

Apple (head) chopped

Thud

Henry, O., from "The Ransom of Red Chief"
  Horse on dirt road; horse whinnies
  Coins
  Cat snarls
  Thud of body
  Metal pan against wood
  Water splashes

Irving, Washington, from "Sleepy Hollow"
  Horse: gallops, plods, whinnies, runs, walks
  Branches rustle, strike wood
  Wildlife: whippoorwill, tree toad, screech
    owl, dog barks, cock crows, cricket
    chirps, bullfrog belch
  Wind
  Whistling

Jacobs, W. W. from "The Monkey's Paw"
  Winds blow
  Footsteps
  Door: knocking, door opens and closes
  Dishes and silverware
  Liquid poured into a glass
  Coins
  Clock ticking
  Match is struck
  Chain rattles
  Chair scrapes on floor and a thud
  Metal bolt creaks and slides open

London, Jack, from "To Light a Fire"
  Rocks
  Bags of gold dust (dirt)
  Bag of coins
  Match is struck
  Fire crackles
  Thin ice cracks (the frozen spittle)
  Dog pants, whines, yips, sounds of
    contentment
  Hands beat on body
  Twigs breaking

**Poe, E. A., from "The Masque of the Red
    Death"**
  Soft thumps (heart beats)
  Knock on door
  Clock clangs
  Bell rings
  Footsteps
  Metal spring collapses (sprung)

Wells, H. G., from "The Country of the Blind"
  Bells ring
  Birds chirp
  Drumming
  Footsteps

About the Author

Photo by Calabash.

Ann N. Black is a native of Iowa and a graduate of Northwestern University, where she received a B.S. from the School of Communication, then worked as an actress and a writer and producer of children's radio dramas. Married to a theatre professor, she, too, switched to the academic life. Her experiences as a critic judge, from directing, teaching, and writing led her to a M.A. in English and Oral Interpretation from the University of North Texas, then to an assistant professorship of literature and creative writing at Northwestern State University of Louisiana. She now lives close to the Rocky Mountains, and, as an enthusiastic member of Society of Children's Book Writers and Illustrators, continues to write for young people. *Born Storytellers: Readers Theatre Celebrates the Lives and Literature of Classic Authors* is her recent companion book of scripts for high school students.

Recent titles in the Readers Theatre series

Character Counts! Promoting Character Education Through Readers Theatre, Grades 2–5
Charla Rene Pfeffinger

Sea Songs: Readers Theatre from the South Pacific
James W. Barnes

Judge for Yourself: Famous American Trials for Readers Theatre
Suzanne I. Barchers

Just Deal with It! Funny Readers Theatre for Life's Not-So-Funny Moments
Diana R. Jenkins

How and Why Stories for Readers Theatre
Judy Wolfman

Born Storytellers: Readers Theatre Celebrates the Lives and Literature of Classic Authors
Ann N. Black

Around the World Through Holidays: Cross Curricular Readers Theatre
Written and Illustrated by Carol Peterson

Wings of Fancy: Using Readers Theatre to Study Fantasy Genre
Joan Garner

Nonfiction Readers Theatre for Beginning Readers
Anthony D. Fredericks

Mother Goose Readers Theatre for Beginning Readers
Anthony D. Fredericks

MORE Frantic Frogs and Other Frankly Fractured Folktales for Readers Theatre
Anthony D. Fredericks

Songs and Rhymes Readers Theatre for Beginning Readers
Anthony D. Fredericks